Battle Ready Finance: Basic Training

Conquer Your Personal Finances in as Little as 8 Weeks

J.W. Zinsmeister
8-23-2013

Legal

Disclaimer

The information contained in this book is for education and informational purposes only. The information should not be misconstrued as financial advice. Your situation is unique and as such you should seek competent professional advice before making any investment decisions. The results you achieve using the information contained in this book will be solely based on your ability and willingness to implement what you have learned. The author does not know you and takes no responsibility for your personal financial situation and cannot guarantee that you will be successful in your financial endeavors. The ideas expressed are based solely on the author's personal experiences and professional training.

Printed in the United States by One Called Writer Publishing – www.oncecalledwriter.com.

ISBN 978-0-61587-025-0

First Edition in the *Battle Ready Finance* Series

TABLE OF CONTENTS

Dedication

If not for the encouragement of my wife Jennifer, the unwavering belief in my writing by Pastor Jerry Lawson, and the hard work of my editors Chris McKinney, Jeb Williamson, Lanie Williamson, Cheri Jones, and Matt Carmichael, as well as graphic artist Jessica Whitmore, this work would have never been completed.

Thank you all for your love, encouragement, and hard work.

Introduction

Like it or not you are in a battle. You were born into a war zone, dropped in behind enemy lines, surrounded by casualties. The enemy is real, the fight is intense, and at stake is your financial future. This war is not fought on distant shores of countries you'll never see. This war is happening all around you and it comes at you from every side. The only chance you have of survival is to become a Battle Ready Financial Warrior.

"Stay alert! Watch out for your great enemy, the devil. He prowls around like a roaring lion, looking for someone to devour." 1 Peter 5:8

Turn a blind eye and deny the reality of the battle and you could well become a prisoner, held captive by debts, haunted by the decision to give in, finding yourself living in a cage of regret.

Stand and fight, and you just might make it out alive, with your self-worth intact, your future secure, and the confidence of a battle tested veteran.

In order to engage the enemy and win, you must first gain the skills necessary to wage war. In this course, you'll learn how to face the enemy head on and to develop the one thing that will ensure your survival above all else. Without knowing this one secret, your chance of success is greatly diminished.

The training you receive will help you survive in battle, thrive in life, and be fearless in the face of the enemy. You'll become familiar with weapons of modern warfare, how to spot the traps that have been set, the fundamentals of close quarters combat, and how to deploy your Secret Weapon. Somewhere inside of you is a Financial Warrior; it is time you two meet.

Welcome to Basic Training.

In the pages that follow, you're going to learn things about money that your parents never taught you. You're going to discover how to develop your Victor-Six-Vision, Learn the Rules of Engagement, build a Battle Ready Budget, and set up Battle Ready Savings. You're going to learn to build Battle Ready Credit and how to deploy your Financial Secret Weapons Arsenal. You're going to see simple ways to lower your stress, eliminate arguments, and regain trust that may have been lost in your marriage due to money issues. If you graduate from Basic Training, your life and your finances will be transformed, putting you on the road to peace and prosperity.

This is not your daddy's war where a sharp eye and a steady hand were enough to earn three squares a day and a nice pension. This is a high tech, fast paced, full-on frontal assault against your money, security, future, and very way of life. You'll need new thinking, specialized weapons, and a shrewd sense of combat to come through unscathed.

Stand up, man up, and join the fight for your family as you take control of your financial life. The world has changed and you need to change with it. Take the necessary step to bulletproof your finances so that when the hot lead and flaming arrows of the enemy start flying, your family will be able to stand firm and fight, while helping others along the way.

In Basic Training, you'll learn the core skills necessary to ensure your finances are Battle Ready.

CHAPTER 1

Develop Battle Ready Vision

"Now faith is the substance of things hoped for, the evidence of things not seen"

_ Once Upon a Time..... _

"I just have this feeling that someday I am going to be very wealthy."

Those were the words of a confident young man once spoken to a young and beautiful college co-ed. While he did have the feeling that he was destined to do great things, there is a slight chance that his desire to convince her he was worth a second glance may have influenced his thinking. He was a naive 21 year old male, full of confidence, and had very little experience with how the world really worked.

Having served in the army and survived the rigors of officer selection and training, he knew for certain there was nothing life could throw at him that he could not overcome. Young, dumb, and full of vigor, the now part time soldier, faced the future with intense confidence.

A college student with limited income but a bright future, he was pursuing a degree in business that would no doubt allow him to land a good job with a fantastic income on which he could begin to build his wealth.

All he really knew about money was when he worked he got paid; if he needed to buy something he paid for it in cash; and he should save some of what he made in case something unexpected comes up.

As simple as that sounds, it was true wisdom. While he had not been taught about money by his parents, he learned that being disciplined with his money allowed him to buy what he needed without much trouble. He did not have much, but he had managed to get through four years of college without needing a single loan.

With hard work and low cost living, he felt sure the future was going to be very prosperous.

With a college degree in hand, something changed in the young man. His thinking on money began to morph into something new. Knowing he had more earning power, the young man began to look at life differently. He felt unstoppable, like he could have whatever he wanted. (Little did he know his change in attitude was planting the seeds that would soon sprout and begin to slowly bear the fruits of stress, tension, and pain.)

After graduation, that young co-ed had indeed believed the young man was worth hanging onto and they were married the following summer. She a nurse and he a business and marketing genius, together they set out to take the world by storm.

Life took off at a blinding pace. Newlyweds with freshly minted degrees, they began building a life together. They dreamed of homes, vacations, and the good life. They talked about kids someday, but knew they wanted to wait and just enjoy getting to know one another for a while. Oddly, the one thing they never really discussed was how to handle their money. It all went into the same account and he paid the bills.

The first mistake he made was buying a new car. Well, buying a new car was not really the mistake; agreeing to pay for it over the next five years would later prove to be a bad decision. In fact, most of the decisions he made about their finances would haunt them for the next decade as they took on one loan after another to finance their wants and needs, all the while "knowing" their incomes would soon catch up and the payments would easily be taken care of each month.

If he were to be honest, our young hero would tell you his insecurity about his new wife, his ignorance about how money really worked, and his confidence in his ability to earn a good wage all conspired against him. He even took it so far as to have a motto about money. Because it made him feel like less of a man to have to tell his new wife they could not afford the things they both wanted, he adopted the motto "Spend All You Want, We'll Make More". Had he truly been a marketing genius, he may have come up with something more original, nevertheless, it was an accurate depiction of the way he viewed his finances.

The problem of course was that unlike the potato chip makers who actually came up with the slogan, he could not make more anytime he wanted. He had no factory to ramp up production, no workers he could put on overtime, and no product he could turn into money. All he had was two salaries, a bunch of bills, and an overgrown ego. He refused to ask for help, to restrict their spending, or to even understand the true problem. Blinded by pride, love, and overconfidence, the couple happily spent all they made and then spent more. The enemy was slowly advancing, undetected and undeterred.

Needless to say, the "Spend All You Want, We'll Make More" mentality led them to a place of struggle and debt they had never intended. Not only did it hurt them financially, it also hurt the quality of their marriage. He began to be less open about finances, less open about his feelings of inadequacy, and less open about his emotions in general.

The way he had handled their money was like a slow acting poison applied to the root of a large tree. First, the effects were not noticeable at all and for a while, things appeared to be fine. Slowly, growth of the relationship stopped. The vibrancy with which they first loved was being replaced by a sinister, seeping rot of deceit, debt, and distrust.

While she was a hard worker and not given to absent minded shopping and spending, he felt he needed to spend money to keep her happy. This was not the case and his inability to talk about it with her left him to act on his faulty assumptions. Mounting bills, missed payments, and the stress of juggling too much month and too little money left him feeling unsatisfied with life and generally unhappy.

Stress, dissatisfaction, and discontent with life became the norm for the young couple and they became more like roommates than husband and wife. Money, or the lack thereof, had become the defining issue of their marriage. As the mistakes stacked on one another like bricks laid by a skilled craftsman, the wall between them grew larger and larger.

There were so many bad financial decisions, so many regrets, so much they wish they could undo. If they had only known then that it would cause them to get so far off track, life could have been different. But like many people, they had to learn the hard way.

He watched the people around him who made less money get nicer homes, better cars, and travel whenever they wanted. He desperately wanted to be like them. Then one day, he made a seemingly harmless decision to become just like them. He got everything they had and did what they did and it was not difficult at all.

He had realized that if he wanted to have and do all those things, all he needed was credit. By simply agreeing that he would make a certain number of monthly payments, he could have almost whatever he wanted.

Need a new car? No worries just finance it for 60 months and it's yours. Need some new furniture? Swipe the card and you can have it. Vacation? No problem. A cash advance and you're off to the beach.

As you may have guessed, the young "hero" in this story is yours truly. I did not know it then, but the enemy and the world system was waging war on our finances and its most devastating weapon was had just unleashed in my life.

Discovering credit was the day that a bad situation turned into a horrible nightmare. Though our "quality of life" improved by common standards, the quality of our future would be greatly diminished. As our incomes grew, the stress of not enough money to buy what we needed was replaced with the vicious cycle of trying to make the revolving payments on all the stuff we wanted.

Under constant siege from enemy forces, we lived in a non-stop cycle for several years. We worked, we spent, we worked, we spent. No budget, no discipline, no savings. Work, spend, work, spend. Wash, rinse, repeat.

After four years of marriage, baby number one came along and we were ecstatic. He was and is a beautiful boy who garnered much of our attention. Of course with a baby comes the need for a crib, a car seat, a bouncy seat, baby clothes, a swing set, baby monitor, potty training seat, baby bed, diaper genie, diapers, diapers, diapers, and more diapers. Who knew babies were so expensive? Probably everyone but me. No problem. I make good money and we've got to have what we've got to have. Work, spend, work, spend.

Funny thing about babies. After you get one, sometimes you want another one. At least, that's what it was like for us. Ah, but this time, we already had all the baby stuff so it should be much cheaper the second time around, right?

Wrong. Baby number two was a girl and as a girl, she could not make use of baby boy clothes and baby boy bedding. She also needed hair bows, dresses for church, Easter, and Christmas. Oh yeah, let's not forget diapers, wipers, creams, and lotions. Did I mention diapers? No problem. Work, spend, work, spend.

With baby number one toddling around and baby number two in diapers, we made the decision for Jennifer to stay home and raise the children. It was a wonderful thing to do and I have no regrets. Our children are well adjusted, well behaved, well-grounded young people and it is in no small part thanks to the sacrifice, time, effort, and love that Jennifer gave. With rising debt, mounting bills, and two new mouths to feed, it was left up to my salary to carry the load. We cut back where we could, made some changes, and got along fine. Work, spend, work spend.

And so it went for a while and all seemed good, except that it wasn't. While we were paying our bills and making ends meet, my job began to take over my life. I would leave before the kids were awake and often get home just in time to put them to bed. Saturdays were spent doing service work or feeling guilty that I was not working.

On the outside, things looked okay, but inside, I was miserable. I began to feel like I was trapped. Trapped by my bills, trapped by my choices, trapped by my skill-set. I felt I had no option except to keep working, keep missing my children grow up, and keep being miserable. I had been taken captive, held in a cage, and was bound by the chains of debt.

No savings meant no options. No margin between my monthly bills and my monthly payment and no way out. I was a prisoner who had walked straight into the enemy trap and volunteered to put on the shackles. Work, spend, work, spend.

I began a desperate search for a way of escape. I considered numerous ways to bring in more money and even tried a few. The net result was frustration, debt, and despair. Finally, with no plan, no savings, and no safety net, I made a break for it. I'd had enough and I wanted out.

Looking back, I should have acted much sooner, should have had a plan ready when I did decide to act, and should have had 3 to 6 months living expenses before I ever considered walking away. But that is not what I did. I just up and quit my job; Wife, two kids, mortgage, car payment, bills, debt and all.

I knew, that regardless of what happened next, it could not be worse than what my life had become. I knew somehow, we would find a way. In other words, I had faith. Not faith in myself. I had already proven I could really make a mess of things. No, I had faith in something bigger than me, something outside of me. Something in my spirit told me it would all be okay. I decided to take a leap and rely on God to work it out. And you know what? He did.

After a two month search, I landed a job with a prestigious firm in an industry in which I had absolutely no experience. While the pay was not great, the training and the flexibility were tremendous. I began an intensive study program in money management and financial planning. I learned about saving, budgeting, investing, and planning for the future in ways that I had never thought about before. I began my own Basic Training.

Having fought the battle for my money entirely unarmed for the last seven years, I had gained a wealth of practical experience in what people should not do with their income. I knew exactly how to relate to people who were frustrated with bills, fed up with taxes, worried about the future, and who wondered if there would ever be a day when they would be free of the worries, the stress, and the despair that accompany money problems.

With new knowledge, new courage, and renewed resolve, we took the fight to the enemy.

Jennifer had begun working the night shift as a nurse which allowed us to pay the bills and with my new training, experience, and some self-study with a popular financial guru, we began to battle our way out. Over the next few years and with the support and assistance of family, we were able to get control of our spending and eliminate $30,000 of credit card debt, which freed Jennifer to leave her position as a night shift nurse. We had escaped from the cage, broken the shackles of debt, and given ourselves a fighting chance. We had broken the work, spend, work, spend cycle.

For us, it started with a desperate need to change our life. I needed to be educated, to learn discipline, and to face the fact that I had put myself in this position. I needed to learn that if things were going to change, then I would have to change them. It all started with a decision and clear vision on what we wanted our future to be. There have still been times along the way where we have fallen victim to old habits, stepped into the same traps of the enemy, and have had to fight our way out. Mistakes are still made and the battle rages on.

While knowing what to do and how to fight is not necessarily the same as doing and fighting, having the knowledge is the first step.

Learning the skills needed to survive against the assaults of the enemy that come against our finances empowers us to make better decisions and gives us the tools to cope with the stress when we don't get it right.

If you can relate to this story at all, then maybe it's time you make a decision of your own. Decide today, that you are tired of living the way you are and you need to make a change. Decide that come hell or high-water, you are going to do what it takes to change your future and the future of your family. Decide to become a Battle Ready Financial Warrior.

You can do this. You must do this. You have a duty to yourself, to your family, to your church, and to your community to be the best you that you can be. The first thing you need is........Vision.

See It In Your Mind to See It in Your Life

"Where there is no vision, the people are unrestrained" Proverbs 29:18

To be successful in battle, you must have a strategy. You must know your enemy's location, tactics, likely point of attack, and weaknesses. You must know your own strengths, capabilities, and competencies. You must be able to match your strengths against the enemy's weaknesses at every opportunity.

In other words, you must have Vision.

Every endeavor great or small starts with a vision. Sometimes well-defined and others a vague idea, a vision of the expected outcome is always present somewhere in the mind. Think of a vision as an idea and you can begin to see that vision is the birthplace of all things.

Every decision you make, every action you take, everything you do, you do because of the vision you carry. It could be a vision you adopted years ago that is still affecting your life. Maybe long ago you were labeled by your friends or family as being shy. Maybe it was even true that you were shy as a child.

However, if you never stop and develop a new vision for yourself, you may go well into your adult life seeing yourself as "the shy one." Because you see yourself as being shy, you naturally act in shy ways. You don't start conversations with new people, you avoid crowds where you might have to socialize and get to know others, and you may even tell yourself that you like being alone. Seeing yourself as shy could have been a vision you adopted in a split second without giving it much thought and now it directs your behavior.

But what if it were not true that you are really shy? What if you actually craved interaction with other people and longed to be outgoing and charismatic but something holds you back?

To get there, the first thing you need to do is change how you see yourself. Change the picture of who you are that you carry around in your head. Envision a new you, re-enforce that belief with yourself regularly, and a new you will begin to emerge.

Your new vision will cause you to begin to think differently about yourself. Your new thoughts will cause you to begin to take different actions. Your new actions will begin to turn into new behaviors. Those new behaviors will become new habits and soon your whole life will be different, all because you adopted a new vision for yourself.

Popular culture media excels at giving us visions of who we should be. A lifetime of TV, movies, songs, and books portraying what success should look like can easily shape the vision that you carry for yourself without you even knowing it has happened. Don't get me wrong, I am not saying that successful people you see on TV or in the movies necessarily make poor role models, I just want you to take some time and examine where YOUR vision of what a successful, happy, well-adjusted you, comes from.

Does it come from what you see around you on TV and in pop culture or is it a well thought out, on purpose, vision for your future born from your own desires, motivations, and internal convictions?

I only ask because no one else ever does.

It's far easier to allow someone else to paint the picture and then just insert yourself in the scene. The problem with this approach is 20 years from now when you step back to look at your masterpiece and you realize it is not your masterpiece at all, rather a cheap imitation of someone else's plan for your life.

Vision shapes everything, and corporate America knows it better than anyone. Companies know if they can get you to picture yourself happy, healthy, and wealthy while using their product, you will begin to adopt their vision of your future. Their vision for your future includes all of the gadgets, luxuries, and stuff they want you to have. Vision is powerful.

Everything you can see, everything you can touch, indeed the entire world is a product of vision. "*In the beginning God created the heavens and the earth*." God had a vision of what He wanted to create before He created anything. In fact, He had a vision of you and your life before He did anything to create the earth. "*Long before he laid down earth's foundations, he had us in mind, had settled on us as the focus of his love, to be made whole and holy by his love.*" Ephesians 1:4

Everything began with God's vision and then He passed the gift of vision on to us, His creation. Created in His image, we have the ability to envision a thing, see it in as much detail as we can imagine, and then follow through until it becomes reality.

He gave us the power to create.

Long ago, someone got tired of sitting on the ground, on rocks, and on uncomfortable pieces of wood. They had envisioned a comfortable place to sit where they could relax and maybe even nap. In their mind's eye they saw a wooden frame with a square base sitting on 4 legs that held the base 18" to 20" above the floor. On one side of the base, two of the legs extend up 24" beyond the top of the base with bracing running horizontally between the legs in a ladder type fashion. The sides, the base, the upper legs, and the bracing are covered with thick foam padding. The whole thing is wrapped in durable yet attractive fabric.

First conceived in the mind as an idea, then nurtured, planned, and developed into a vision, the upholstered chair was born. Later, someone else envisioned being able to lean back in the chair without falling over, possibly to take a nap. Not satisfied with leaning the chair against the wall at a 45 degree angle (they probably had a mean older brother who kept kicking the chair out from under them as they napped), the reclining, overstuffed man chair came to life.

As so it is with all things. Nothing happens without first an idea. Nothing good and lasting happens without that idea growing into a vision.

Some visions are well thought out, well planned, and well executed. They are intentional and rational causing the eventual outcome to be almost assured. The vision, once firmly rooted in the mind, compels you to take actions that move you closer to the realization of the vision. With a vision of what you want to accomplish, you become aware of which things are moving you closer to the desired outcome and which are moving you further away. If the vision is clear enough, doing only the things that work toward the vision becomes your natural behavior and soon the vision is reality.

What happens when there is no vision?

Someone once said "If you don't know where you're going, anywhere will do". If you have no vision for the future, no plan of action, no goal in mind, then you'll get whatever results chance and time happen to deliver. You may stumble upon success or fall headlong into failure. You may make great gains or lag further behind. You may charge up the hill and take it with ease or be repelled by blows from your opponent. Without a vision, all bets are off.

In the absence of a clear vision of the outcome you desire, your daily decisions and actions become only those that satisfy you at that moment. Proverbs says *"Without vision, the people are unrestrained."* Unrestrained in their behavior because there is no motivation to do anything other than what feels good. No eye to the future, no thought of the consequences, and no accountability for the results.

Without a vision for the desired outcome, chances are slim the outcome will be to your liking. In fact, another translation of the same verse in Proverbs says *"without vision, the people perish."*

In the battle for your finances, lack of vision can bring with it death. Death of relationships, death of financial order, death of hopes and dreams, death of the abundant life.

In combat, both spiritual and physical, a lack of vision can be devastating.

Imagine yourself as a soldier on a real battlefield. You are summoned in the early morning hours and darkness hangs thick in the air. Surrounded by your fellow troops, you sense the uneasy tension as you wait for orders.

Just then, a young Lieutenant walks up. "Alright men, listen up. Out there, somewhere up ahead is the enemy. We don't know how many there are, what kind of weapons they have, exactly where they are located, and we're not sure what they look like." As you begin to wonder just what you have gotten yourself into, the young Lt. continues. "Here's what I want you to do. Assemble your squads, march out into the jungle, and engage the enemy. Just remember, there are probably land mines, booby traps, and most likely you will be ambushed." "Umm, Sir? What kind of terrain will we be crossing?" asks a soldier from the back. "Not sure" came the Lieutenant's reply. "We've been so busy getting tomorrow's entertainment lined up that we really haven't had time to send out scouts. But don't worry; I'm sure you'll be fine. Let me know when you get back. Now, move out."

On the battlefield, a lack of vision equals almost certain death.

While it's a ridiculous scenario that would never happen, a very similar experience happens daily in the lives of millions of people. They navigate life with no plan, no destination, and no idea of what's waiting in the darkness. Concerned about only today and consumed with a constant blitz of meaningless chatter about the lives of celebrities, they blissfully bounce along life's highway oblivious to the obstacles that lie ahead.

But not you. The mere fact that you are reading this book says that you want to know where you are headed. You want to walk forward in confidence, knowing that you have the training and tools to succeed. You want to be fully armed and prepared for the battle. All you need now is the right kind of vision.

You need Battlefield Vision.

Victor-Six-Vision

Developing a vision that will serve you well takes intention. It is something you must do on purpose. To ensure that your vision will remain at the forefront of your mind, I am going to teach you how to create a six sided vision called a Victor-Six-Vision.

To avoid confusion in combat, individual letters are given names such as Victor for the letter V or Papa for the letter P. In the heat of battle, you do not want the boys calling in the airstrike to confuse your C's and D's with P's and V's. Naming the letters keeps you from being killed by your fellow troops.

Naming your vision will also help keep your finances alive. Knowing you have a purpose and an outcome to achieve that is well defined and easily communicated allows you to stay on track and keep those around you in the loop. To be effective, you need a Victor-Six Vision. You could call it V-6 if you prefer, but Victor-Six-Vision sounds more like a mission and less like a bingo number.

So what is a Victor-Six-Vision?

A Victor-Six is a Vision that is characterized by having the following six attributes:

It must be Vital; it must be Viable; it must be Valuable; it must be Vivid; you must be able to Verbalize it; and it must be Verifiable.

A well-crafted Victor-Six will include your mission statement, desired goals, and internal motivation. It will define the desired outcome in a way that will allow anyone involved to instantly understand what is being sought in order to join the fight as they have opportunity.

Let's take a look at each of the six attributes and see how they can help make your vision one that continually drives your behavior, spurs you on toward the outcome you desire, and helps those around your understand and support your mission.

It Must Be Vital

"May He give you what your heart desires and fulfill your whole purpose." Psalm 20:4

The first component of your Victor-Six is that it must be Vital. That is to say, it must be important to you and your family. A vital vision is one that has the power to positively change your life and the lives of those around you. Your vision needs to be one that if you fail to realize it, your life will be lacking in some way that is critical to you. The key part is that it is a vision that is important to YOU.

I am not talking about a vision that someone has told you is right for you. Not a vision for your future you have read in a book or saw on TV.

This is your personal vision for your life that you have taken time to think through, develop, and believe. This is a vision that because of its vast importance to you and what it would mean in your life, you will stop at nothing until it is realized.

In the fight for your finances, you are the battlefield commander. You choose the mission. This is Your vision.

A vital financial vision could be one centered on the amount of income you earn. Let's say you currently earn $2000 per month but you can envision earning $5000 per month. The first step in making this vision vital is to ask yourself why making $5000 per month is important to you? What does it do for you? What does having the extra money mean to your life? What impact will it have on your family? How will it change your life for the better? What will happen if you don't get there? Answer these questions and you are well on your way to developing a vital vision.

To understand why it is vital, you should take time to think through the answers and write them down. Answering the questions for this $2000 to $5000 increase in income might look like this:

1. Why is making $5000 per month important to me?

- By bringing home an extra $3000 per month in income, we can begin to pay down our debts. Paying down our debts will lower our stress, ease the tension in our marriage, and allow us to begin to think more clearly about the future.

2. What does making $5000 per month do for me personally?

- It will make it easier for me to sleep at night knowing that I am paying my bills and regaining some ground. I worry a lot about our debt and the sooner it is gone, the less I will have to worry about.

3. What does having the extra money mean in my life?

- Besides just paying off debt, being able to earn $3000 more per month would give me a sense of accomplishment, build my confidence, and allow me to feel better about myself by knowing I can provide for my family. Knowing I can fulfill my role as husband, dad, and provider would bring a sense of satisfaction with my life that is missing.

4. What impact will it have on my family?

-When I am stressed and worried about money, I am not able to fully be present with my wife and children. I am always preoccupied with financial matters. Bringing in the extra money will help me to refocus and reengage with my family and will improve our time we spend together.

5. How will it change your life for the better?

-Making $3000 extra per month and applying it to our debt for 12 months will allow us to get rid of all consumer debt. Once we are free from the debt, we can save for and take vacations without feeling guilty. We can begin to save for the kids college, or retirement, or a better car. We can explore what God really wants us to do with our lives. The extra money will give us options and flexibility.

6. What will happen if I don't get there?

-If I am not able to earn the extra money, I will continue to feel stuck. My stress level will remain high, impacting my health, my family life, and all of my relationships. The debts we have continually punch me in the guts and I must begin to fight back. Living in debt has become almost unbearable and continuing for another five years this way is not an option.

Those six questions, if asked and answered honestly, will put you well on your way to working out the vision in a way that is vital to you.

It Must Be Viable

"I assure you: If anyone says to this mountain, 'Be lifted up and thrown into the sea,' and does not doubt in his heart, but believes that what he says will happen, it will be done for him." Mark 11:23

Your vision also must be Viable. It must be one that you truly can believe in order for it to happen. If you develop a vision to become a millionaire in 12 months but you have never known a person who has done it, have no skills that could lead to it, have not designed a plan that can deliver those results, have not heard from God that He will do it, and have no idea of how that could be accomplished, then for you, that vision is not viable at the moment.

While you don't need to have all of the answers as to how you will make it happen, you must at least be working toward a vision that is reality based. You don't have to know every step in the plan. You don't even have to know another person who has realized a similar vision. **But you do have to believe you can do it, and believe it with everything you've got.**

A viable vision is one that, while you can't necessarily see exactly how it is going to happen, you have enough faith in yourself and faith in God to believe that it will happen. You need to know if you do all you can do and work toward the outcome with purpose and intention, it's only a matter of time until the vision will become a reality. That knowledge you have deep down in your spirit that you can make it is the key ingredient to developing a viable vision.

Viable does not always have to mean reasonable. Viable can mean outlandish, crazy, not-gonna-happen-unless-God-makes-it-happen, but I have enough faith to believe for it anyway kind of vision. It's okay to stretch yourself, to exercise your faith muscles and believe for more. In fact, it's better than okay, it's preferred. The best and most viable visions are the ones that scare you at first and make other people think you're a few bullets shy of a full magazine.

Big visions bring emotion to the equation and emotion is a force multiplier. When you have developed a big vision, fully believe that somehow it is going to happen, and you embrace the fear and uncertainty with a calm resolve, God makes things conspire to work in your favor. Bind your emotions to your belief, your belief to your will, and your will to your actions, and the world will begin to reshape to see your vision realized.

As powerful as being vital and viable are, your vision is still just hitting on two cylinders. A Victor-two may eventually get you where you want to go, but it will be slow and noisy and you'll burn a lot of oil. Add the other four Victors to crank up the power.

It Must Be Valuable

"I, Yahweh, have called You for a righteous purpose, and I will hold You by Your hand." Isaiah 42:6

Once you have developed a vision that is both vital and viable, it is time to ensure it is also valuable.

While you may think having a vital vision automatically makes it valuable, I want you to think through the differences for a moment. We said earlier that a vital vision is one that is critical to you and your family, but does that necessarily make it valuable to you? The easy answer is "Of course it makes it valuable. I love my family and I want the best for them."

While I have no doubt that is true, it still does not get down to the core issue. You see, as humans, we have the capacity to recognize something as being vital without assigning enough value for it to cause us to act.

For instance, I may feel it is vital for my own well-being that I find a way to lose weight and get my cholesterol under control. In fact, the doctor may have even told me if I don't do something, I may not be around to see my grandchildren. Is that vital? Sure it is. But until I place more value on becoming healthy than I do on having the right to enjoy whatever food I want in quantities that make me happy, I will continue the same lifestyle.

Just because it is vital, does not always mean it will cause you to do what must be done.

How many people in the world understand how vital it is for lung health that they do not smoke yet place more value on the feeling they get from smoking than from knowing they have healthy lungs?

How many times have you spent money knowing you should not spend it, yet you placed more value on getting what you wanted than on saving or paying off debt?

How many times has there been a need in your church or your community that was vitally important and would change lives but it went unfunded because people could not see the value in giving?

How valuable we make our vision in our mind will have a direct impact on how soon, if ever, the vision is realized. The amount of value you place on your vision must be high enough to override the things that compete for the resources you need to realize it.

In order to have a valuable vision, you have to get really, really honest with yourself. You have to reach down into places that you don't really like, deep down in places you don't talk about at parties (I wrote that in my best Jack Nicholson voice) and see what you're holding onto as valuable that might get in the way.

I highly value the ability to be in complete control of how I spend my time. As a Financial Consultant, I get to make my own schedule, work as many or as few hours as I choose, and take as long of a lunch break as I see fit. I also value earning a good paycheck. When short hours and long lunches begin to translate into lower take home pay, I have a choice. I can decide that I place more value on playing golf on a Tuesday and I am okay with making less money. If that lines up with my Vision and I can still support my family, then golf on Tuesday can be a great way for me to recharge while entertaining clients and prospects.

Conversely, I can decide that making less money is for the birds and I had better get my tail back to work.

If my Victor-Six-Vision is to earn more money per month in order to better my family, pay off my debts, decrease my stress, and help me to be a better father, the choice is easy. Because I have made my vision more valuable than playing golf on Tuesdays, I will go to work.

The key for making sure your vision is valuable is to assign the value before the things that compete with it come up.

Suppose you know you have a weakness for shoes. It's so bad, you can't even drive by a shoe store without getting caught in its gravitational pull and coming out with a new pair of TOM's. Your goal is to save $100 per week to buy a new used car in 36 months. Your current car is just above the clunker category and you would like to upgrade to the still-embarrasses-the-kids-but-just-barely category.

When should you make the decision that the 18 pairs of TOM's you have in your closet are enough and you are not going to buy anymore? Would it be better to make that decision as you are summoned from the car by the music and balloons at the Shoe Carnival? Should you wait until you are in the store enjoying that new shoe smell?

Chances are waiting until you can see the whites of the shoe store manager's eyes before deciding not to spend the money will be less than effective. Instead, you must convince yourself of the value of saving for the next car.

You must have total buy-in to your vision and have decided beforehand you are not going to buy another pair of shoes until you can drive your new car and pick them out.

Be firm and resolute, knowing your vision is Vital, Viable, and Valuable, and a little pair of dainty shoes with folded over toes is not going to get in your way.

It Must Be Vivid

"Make yourself an ark of gopher wood. Make rooms in the ark, and cover it with pitch inside and outside. This is how you are to make it: The ark will be 450 feet long, 75 feet wide, and 45 feet high. You are to make a roof, finishing the sides of the ark to within 18 inches of the roof. You are to put a door in the side of the ark. Make it with lower, middle, and upper decks." Genesis 6:14-16

Next, you must make your vision Vivid. A vivid vision is one that is fully thought out in as much detail as you can muster and is painted in living color on the screen of your mind. In your mind's eye, you should see it, feel it, hear it, smell it, and taste it, just as you would if it were your real life.

On the battlefield, sand tables are used to make the upcoming battles as vivid as possible. Combat leaders gather around tables with a sand top. In the sand, the battlefield is laid out for everyone to see. The terrain is simulated and troop positions are designated by figures representing squad or platoon size elements. Enemy positions are placed where the latest intel says they are located. Minefields are noted and the scene is set.

The leaders strategize the best way to attack, look for defensive positions, and determine where each of their assets should be deployed. They move the troops on the sand table into position, anticipate the enemy's reactions, and develop strategies of response. The battle is carried out over and over on the sand table until each leader knows exactly what is expected. Only when they all have a clear vision of the outcome do they act.

With the vision intact, the actions on the battlefield will support the vision and all guesswork is removed.

You need a sand table of your own. You need to run the battle in your mind until you begin to see the outcome you want. You should see yourself living in the place that your vision will take you, enjoying the life that you desire, and doing what God has called you to do. You should replay this film in your mind as often as you can.

When you become convinced in your mind the vision is becoming your reality and you believe it without doubt, your actions will start to change to support the vision.

Your thoughts drive your actions, your actions become habits, and your habitual behavior will soon see your desired outcome achieved.

Just as having a vivid vision will drive your behavior, eliminate guesswork, and give you the best chance for victory, a foggy, unclear vision increases the chance your enemy will inflict heavy damages.

Let's assume you currently have little savings, no retirement, are living paycheck to paycheck, and long for something different. In that circumstance, what you feed your mind will make a huge and lasting impact on the outcome you eventually see.

If you dwell on the fact that you have no money and will never retire, you will eventually start to believe there is no use in even trying. Your thoughts will be those of poverty. You will feel there is no hope. As a result, your automatic behavior will be to keep spending and keep living paycheck to paycheck. Saving will become almost impossible. Your automatic behavior will turn into life-long habits and your habitual behavior will dictate the vision you have been giving yourself of staying stuck soon becomes your lasting reality.

The great news is the opposite is also true. When you form a vivid vision of what you want your life to look like and you truly believe it will happen, your thoughts begin to change. Because your thoughts drive your actions, your actions begin to change. *"As a man thinks in his heart, so is he" Prov 23:7.* As you keep the vision alive and at the front of your mind, your actions become habits. Before long, you are acting to support your vision out of habit and you are well on your way to seeing the vision realized.

When the vision is vital, viable, valuable, and vivid, you become an unstoppable force that no enemy can repel. Split second decisions made in the heat of battle will be the right decisions only when the vision is clear.

It Must Be Verbalized

"The Lord said, 'If they have begun to do this as one people all having the same language, then nothing they plan to do will be impossible for them'." Genesis 11:6

As the vision takes shape, you must begin to verbalize your vision as often as you can. You must speak it out loud to yourself and to those around you.

While you may find this awkward and receive some less than positive feedback, don't let that stop you. Your vision must be on your lips any time you talk about your situation. Proverbs says that "the power of life and death is in the tongue" and nowhere is it more important than when you are speaking about the direction of your life. You have a choice to speak blessings and hope over your life or doom and despair.

You can say things like "I'm just so far in debt I'll never get ahead". You can say "I'm no good at managing money and I'm always broke. You can speak those words over yourself so often that soon you can believe nothing else. The power to cause death is in your tongue and you are using it against yourself.

Or you can choose to speak in faith.

You can say "I have a plan, I have faith, and I have a God that has promised to never leave me or forsake me and because of that, I know I will get my debts paid off and my financial house will be put in order." You can choose to say "It may not look like it now, but I am on my way to the top of my industry. Before long, people will be coming to me for advice about money. I am a turnaround story. I have a vision, and I have a hope, and nothing will stand in my way." Speak life into your circumstances.

When Jesus walked the earth, He modeled this over and over throughout His ministry. More than 200 times in the New Testament, the word "say" is used when giving instructions on how we are to live and act. Probably the most recognizable is Mark 11:23: "*I tell you the truth, you can say to this mountain, 'May you be lifted up and thrown into the sea,' and it will happen. But you must really believe it will happen and have no doubt in your heart.*"

Your words have power. Stop telling people how big your mountains are and start telling your mountains how big your God is.

Talk to yourself like that and see if things don't start to change. Motivate yourself to take action and leave the fear and doubt behind. You may still stumble, you may have setbacks, but drive on. Keep fighting and soon the momentum will shift. Take the next hill and stand your ground.

Verbalizing your vision the right way allows you to take enemy ground and advance your vision. At the very least, you will be a much more enjoyable person to be around.

It Must Be Verifiable

"God saw all that He had made, and it was very good."
Genesis 1:31

Finally, the vision must be verifiable.

Your vision should be clear enough that you will be able to know when you have achieved it or when you have made significant progress. You should have benchmarks along the way to verify you are on the right path. Look at the map of your financial future and draw a line in the sand. That is your next target. Advance until you hit that line and then refuse to go back. Use the lines to verify your progress and to know that your vision is becoming a reality.

A vision centered on "I want to have more money" is one that can never be verified yet can always be verified. The first day you have a dollar more than you had yesterday, you will have "more money" and the vision is achieved. Except that because the vision was that you "want" more money, you can never verify when you have satisfied the want.

A verifiable vision is one that has a specific set of targets that when hit, can be celebrated and rewarded.

You have a vision to pay off your debt. Sounds good, but is it verifiable? Sure it is, when all of your debt is paid off. But what if you got more specific?

Assume you decided that in your Victor-Six-Vision, you were going to pay off your smallest debt in one month and then add that payment to your next debt. In one months' time, you would be able to verify that you had stuck to the plan and paid off the debt. You could choose to celebrate and reward yourself as a way to drive you on to the next verifiable point. A verifiable vision is one that has a definite end goal in mind.

A good vision will give you a direction to travel and a goal to accomplish.

A great vision will not only give you a direction and a goal, it will add purpose and meaning to your decisions.

A Victor-Six-Vision will give you direction, set benchmarks along the way, add purpose to your decisions, add meaning to your life, drive your behavior, and inspire those around you to help you accomplish your vision in any way they can.

That's the power of a Victor-Six.

As an example, here is the Victor-Six I developed as a guide to help with the writing of this series of books:

> In the next 8 months I will write, edit, and produce a series of 4 books on sound money management that teach other people what they need to know to improve their finances based on where they are currently in their lives. (*Verifiable*) Every day, I get out of bed at 5:00 and write, seeing the books take shape as the words come easily. (*Verifiable*) In these books I teach about developing good financial habits, covering everything from basic savings to advanced concepts of legacy giving, teaching the topics relevant to people at different times in their financial journey. (*Vivid*) Writing is important to me as it allows me to fill a deep need to use my gifts to reach as many people as possible. (*Vital*) In addition to changing the way people think about and handle their money, the books encourage them to become givers, even extravagant givers, as well as give them the tools and know how to do so. By doing this, I am able to help churches and other non-profits increase the amount of tithes, offerings, and long term gifts they receive. As a result they carry the gospel message to more people, save more souls, impact more lives, and spread the word of God to a lost and dying world. (*Valuable*) These books are available to churches and individuals around the country and even the world. They launch a new ministry that gives

me a larger platform from which to reach more people. (*Viable*) These books address one of the largest and most damaging problems of our time: poor Financial Stewardship. Mishandling money has enslaved more people than physical chains. I teach people to break free of those chains and take back control of their lives so they may fully surrender to do the work God has called them to do and become the people they were meant to be. (*Vivid*) My books are a force for God, beating back the advance of the enemy for the cause of Christ, and the gates of hell will not prevail against the work I have been called to do. (*Verbalize*) Together with my brothers and sisters in Christ, we are taking back what the devil and his schemes have stolen, regaining control of our money, and using it as a tool to advance Gods kingdom for His glory. (*Vital*) I am called to take up this battle, to step into the fray, and to build others up to fight, and I will not fail. (*Valuable*) I can do all things through Christ who strengthens me. (*Verbalize*)

I keep my Victor-Six near my bed, posted at my desk at work, and have it on my iPad to read as often as possible. Keeping it always in front of me drives me to complete the work I have set out to do. If I want to sleep in and skip a day of writing, my Victor-Six reminds me that the decision has already been made to wake up and write. If I start to feel like it is too much and can't be done, my Victor-Six reminds me it is what I am called to do and because I am called, I am also empowered. If I begin to feel selfish and want to do other things, my Victor-Six reminds me that it is not about me. My Victor-Six guides my thinking, drives my actions, builds my habits, and drives my vision to completion.

Battle Ready Training Task 1.1

Develop Your Victor-Six-Vision

Alright solider, time for your first challenge. You have a dream, something you want to accomplish. You want to gain control of your money, pay off your debt, save for a house, or any of a hundred other things. Whatever it is, it is yours.

To move it from dream to reality, you need your own Victor-Six.

This is your first Battle Ready Training Task. Answer the following questions in as much detail as possible and then, using the answers, craft your own Victor-Six:

What exactly is the outcome you want to achieve?

What is the thing you want to accomplish?

Make it Vivid

1) What does it look like in your life?

2) What does it feel like once you have achieved it?

3) What will change in your life as a result?

4) What do you see when you look around?

5) What do you hear being said about you by your peers?

6) What changes does it make in other people?

Make it Vital

1) Why is it important?

2) What will it do for you?

3) What does it mean in your life?

4) What impact will it have on your family?

5) How will it change your life for the better?

6) What will happen if you don't get there?

Make it Valuable

1) How important is this outcome to you?

2) What other things will compete for resources?

3) What sacrifices will need to be made?

4) Are you willing to say no to some good?

Make it Viable

1) Are you truly convinced this can happen?

2) Have you found scriptures that support your vision?

3) Do you believe this outcome lines up with God's will?

4) Does this outcome require special skills?

5) Do you know another person who has been successful?

6) Do you have buy-in from your spouse?

Make it Verifiable

1) How will you know you are making progress?

2) Draw a line in the sand to set an intermediate target.

3) Can you measure your progress in more than one way?

4) What is the end outcome you are fighting for?

Make it Verbal

1) Can it be distilled into one paragraph?

2) Are you bold enough to share your Victor-Six with others?

3) Can you print it on a card to refer to often?

4) Does speaking it out loud encourage you?

5) When you hear yourself say it, do you believe it?

Once you have answered these questions, compile the answers in a way that is pleasing to you. It could be a narrative like the Victor-Six I wrote for this book, it could be in bullet points, it could be written on a series of note cards.

Whatever form it takes, take ownership. This is Your Victor-Six and it will guide you along this journey as you fight from victory to victory.

DO NOT PROGRESS ANY FURTHER IN THIS BOOK UNTIL YOU HAVE TAKEN THE TIME TO DEVELOP YOUR OWN VICTOR-SIX-VISION.

It's not hard to do, it is a critical component of your success, and you owe it to yourself to do it.

Now, get busy.

Chapter 2

Determine Your Battle Ready Rules of Engagement

"March around the city with all the men of war, circling the city one time. Do this for six days. Have seven priests carry seven ram's-horn trumpets in front of the ark. But on the seventh day, march around the city seven times, while the priests blow the trumpets. When there is a prolonged blast of the horn and you hear its sound, have all the people give a mighty shout. Then the city wall will collapse, and the people will advance, each man straight ahead." Joshua 6:3-5

Definition: Rules of Engagement (ROE) are rules or directives to military forces (including individuals) that define the circumstances, conditions, degree, and manner in which force, or actions which might be construed as ambiguous, may be applied. They provide authorization for and/or limits on, among other things, the use of force and the employment of certain specific capabilities.

With the vision intact and the outcome set firmly in mind, it's time to learn the rules. While it has often been said that all is fair in love and war, implying that there are no rules to follow, the reality is quite different.

In every military campaign, decisions must be made regarding when to attack, when to evade, when to advance, and when to pull back. Just as the Victor-Six is developed before taking the battlefield, so too must the Rules of Engagement be clearly determined. The troops on the ground must know what to do when they encounter enemy forces and these decisions have to be made before the conflict begins.

In the Battle of Jericho, God clearly established the rules for Joshua and his men. Some of the men may have wanted to run and hide. Others may have wanted to storm the gates and attack head on. But God laid down the Rules of Engagement and by following the rules, Joshua and his men were successful in battle.

The same is true for your fight. You must determine many things about how to handle your money before the situation arises. While every situation cannot be known ahead of time and some may take you by surprise, many can be anticipated. Knowing when to pay cash, when to write a check, when to say no thanks, when to postpone the purchase, when to say yes, and when to have a discussion before buying will save you and your spouse a lot of heartache and stress and will help build or reestablish trust.

A well established, clearly developed, and adequately communicated Victor-Six will be the overarching framework from which you operate and the Rules of Engagement (ROE) will act in concert to support the Victor-Six. Having to make the same decision multiple times is inefficient, ineffective, and an invitation for disaster. A well-developed set of Rules of Engagement can put decision making on automatic.

Before deployment, soldiers are briefed on what to do when they come in contact with the enemy. While you may think that sounds strange, it is quite necessary. A soldier's job is not always to fight. Sometimes, it is better to remain concealed and observe. Sometimes is it better to exit the area undetected and report back to higher command. Sometimes, engaging in a firefight is the right choice. Those decisions, when made before the battle begins and clearly understood by all involved, save lives, save time, and support the Victor-Six-Vision for the desired outcome of the conflict.

A clear set of Financial Rules of Engagement that are well thought out, clearly communicated, and agreed to by all parties are an absolute necessity for a Battle Ready Financial Warrior.

So, what are the rules?

That's up to you, the Battlefield Commander, to decide. This is your fight and you know your strengths and weaknesses. You know many of the tactics of the enemy that have been successful against you in the past and what may be used again. Your ROE may be very different from mine or anyone else and they must be specific to your fight.

However, there are some common ROE that will serve most families well. Consider these and add your own as you see fit.

ROE # 1

Never use mistakes to beat your fellow soldier.

Squads are like families. They live together, train together, fight together, and make mistakes together. Nothing is more damaging to squad cohesiveness as an unforgiving squad member constantly bringing up mistakes of others. A good leader does not tolerate such behavior and will stand and defend all those under his charge, even against one of their own.

You must do the same in your family. You cannot allow anyone to abuse another with their financial mistakes. Nothing good will come from such behavior. If someone has messed up, dug a hole, and you have all fallen in, the best course of action is to stop digging and work together to find a way out. Reminding them they dug the hole in the first place will get you nowhere. Correct the behavior and move on. Learn the lesson and let it go.

If you want to destroy your chances of seeing your Victor-Six realized, just follow this pattern: each time money is mentioned, remind yourself or the other person of the failings that have caused your financial struggle. Recall all of the times they messed up, recounting each case with dollar amounts included. Be sure and tell them they cannot manage money at all and are sure to make the same mistakes again. Be relentless, be unforgiving, and you will soon find your situation is even worse.

To see your Victor-Six realized, strive to inspire others to do more, be more, and accomplish more than they ever thought possible.

Rather than reminding them of the mistakes of the past, speak in a way that conveys you believe in them, you are working with them, and together you will succeed.

When you talk about a person who has had a spending problem, don't bring it up. Instead, speak of how they are learning so much about money, the great habits they are developing, the good steward they are becoming, the good decisions they are beginning to make, and the progress that is being achieved.

Speak words of life, words of encouragement, and words of hope to each other. Speak words of life to yourself, out loud, for you to hear. Thoughts are fleeting and will betray you. Hearing words of life spoken by you or another will cement the ideas in your mind and bring faster, better results.

ROE # 2

Determine the method by which you will operate.

Cash in hand or debit card? Check or credit? How will you pay for everyday items like gas, food on the go, and coffee? Decide your method and then stick to it regardless of the situation.

Should you decide, and all parties agree, that the cash method is the best way to operate, take steps to ensure cash is available when needed. Keep enough cash on hand to cover your purchases but not so much that you will be tempted to buy unneeded items. If debit cards are your chosen method, take steps to ensure there is cash in the bank to support the purchase.

Don't overlook this rule. Danger lies around every corner waiting to catch you off guard and overwhelm you. Pay attention, stay alert, and stay alive. Know your habits, your weaknesses and those of your family.

Every day you are out of your home, there is a good chance you will need money. Your car will need gas once a week or at least a few times a month. To fill the tank could be as much as $60, depending on the vehicle, maybe more. How will you pay? How will your spouse or your children with cars pay?

While you may think this is a small decision, I can assure you it is not. Assuming there are two adult drivers in your home who both require one tank of gas per week and the average fill up is $50, how much would that cost in a year?

Two tanks of gas a week at $50 per tank for 50 weeks (or 52 if you never slow down) equal $5,000 per year. For any large purchase, either cumulative or all at one time, you should have a rule in place. Without a ROE for this situation, you could easily charge $2,000 to $5,000 per year on a credit card without even realizing the impact. Ask me how I know.

How about lunch? It's only $5 a day for fast food or $8 to $10 for a single meal at a diner. No big deal, right?

One person eating out for $8.00 a day for 50 weeks is $2,000. Two adults eating out a day and two kids eating school lunches can easily put that number at close to $5,000.

A Battle Ready Financial Warrior will know where that money is going to come from. Mindless spending, that is spending without giving it a second thought because it is only a few dollars, given enough time will wreck your finances. Ask me how I know.

Establishing the method by which daily purchases will be made just makes sense. If you use a debit card, your wife writes checks, and you both hand cash to the kids as needed, money will begin to run through your hands like water. Choose to always pay with cash whenever possible and statistics show that you will spend an average of 20% less as you navigate life. Plug the leaks, agree on a plan, and you will benefit from knowing how money is walking out your door. You may not be able to convince it to stay, but at least you can wish it well as it's leaving.

ROE # 3

Determine what amount of money can be spent without a conversation.

Every family should discuss the amount of money each person is allowed to spend before consenting adults need to get together and have a conversation. This one rule will do more to alleviate stress, reduce arguments, and keep you on track than all other ROE. Every person in your home who spends money should know this rule inside and out and agree to stick to it.

How much is your spending limit? Well, that's up to you to decide. Some families may decide that for non-routine purchases no one should spend more than $50 without first talking it over with their spouse. Some may decide the limit is $30. For others, it could be $100 or $1000. Whatever the number is for you, make a decision and agree to abide by it.

This rule is all about trust and accountability and not about dollar amounts. The dollar amounts are flexible and can change as needed. Trust is not. Trust must be established and reinforced with daily actions.

Consider a typical family. The weather is turning warmer and summer is just around the corner. The outdoors begins to call. Fishing weather is here and dad needs a new fishing rod. He knows they really can't afford to splurge right now, but he wants that new rod and reel. Besides, he works hard and he deserves it. He knows if he buys it and his wife finds out, a fight will soon follow. To avoid conflict, dad decides to dip into his "mad money" he has been secretly stashing away for just such occasions. He plops down the $129.99 for the new rod and reel combo and sets fire to the receipt. When he gets home, he slips it over into his bass boat and looks forward to the weekend.

Meanwhile, the weather has mom in a spending mood too. She knows the kids will need new clothes for the winter and now is the perfect time to find great deals and maybe even pick up a few things for her along the way. With no "mad money" of her own, mom relies on store credit cards. The bills are in her name and she pays them as soon as they come in the mail. Besides, it's not like she's hiding anything. The kids do *need* those clothes.

After a few hours of shopping, mom finds several great buys for the whole family and even though she spent $250, in her mind she saved almost $100 by being a savvy shopper. Mom heads home and hangs the new clothes in the closets and may decide at dinner to mention that she picked up a few things for the kids.

You could argue that mom and dad are not really out to deceive each other. Both could justify their purchases and for the sake of peace, they decided it is better to just get what is needed. After all, it's really not *that much* money. Right?

The problems with this approach are numerous, but let's just hit the big ones.

First, there is a total lack of communication. No one knows what the other is doing. Without communication, the partnership begins to suffer. When couples no longer feel like partners, trust starts to fade. When trust is gone, the enemy has you right where he wants you.

Looking purely at the numbers, collectively mom and dad spent $379.00 plus tax. If they engage in similar behavior just 4 times a year, they will have spent $1,652 without ever having talked about where the money would come from or how it would be used.

What should they do differently?

I recommend that mom and dad decide on a set of ROE and agree to only spend $100.00 before they needed to run it by the other one. Not to get permission, not so they could beat each other up over things they need and want, but just so the other party is given the courtesy of being kept in the loop.

While dad was at the fishing store and knowing that ROE # 3 had been established, he would have had a few options. First, he could look at lower priced rod and reel combos to stay under the $100.00 mark. Failing that, he could call his wife and make her aware of his intentions.

How that conversation goes will be based on their personalities, their current financial position, and the status of their relationship. However it goes, the important thing is to have the conversation. As long as you keep Rule #1 (Never use mistakes to beat your fellow soldier) in mind, talking about spending the money will build trust, foster communication, and solidify the partnership that you agreed to when you married.

The same holds true for mom. While she could easily justify buying clothes for the children at good prices, merely talking it over with her husband before she makes the purchases shows a great deal of respect and will build honesty in their relationship.

None of this is to say that mom and dad should not spend money on things they want and need, just that they should agree to talk about it first. If they both agree there is a need and spending the money supports the Victor-Six they can move forward knowing they are still on track.

While ROE are important for couples they are just as important for singles. You may not have another person you are accountable to, but you are accountable to yourself and your Victor-Six. Set a spending limit that you will abide by and don't go over it without due consideration of what you are trying to accomplish.

Does the purchase get you closer to your outcome or push you further away? If you still have the urge to spend, step away for a cooling off period of 24-48 hours and then come back to the decision. Chances are you will make a much better choice after a little time has passed.

As you progress further along in your Battle Ready mindset, you will discover the ROE you established rarely come into play.

When your Victor-Six-Vision is strong enough, well communicated, and you have total buy in, you will already know if buying a new fishing rod supports your vision or goes against it. Without even thinking about what you should do, you will know the right answer. When the behavior that supports the Victor-Six becomes automatic, you are well on your way to becoming a Battle Ready Financial Warrior.

Until then, follow your ROE to the letter and you can't go wrong.

ROE # 4

Determine how you will respond when rules are broken.

Sooner or later you will mess up. You'll slip. You'll spend money you shouldn't spend, buy something you don't need, or do something with your money that you will regret. If not you, then someone in your home. It happens. We don't want it to happen, we don't plan for it to happen, and we may not even understand why it happened. It's called being human. *"For what I am doing, I do not understand; for I am not practicing what I would like to do, but I am doing the very thing I hate."* Romans 7:15

When this occurs, the first thing to do is remain calm. Overreacting now is what the enemy is counting on. It's one of his traps to trip you up and to bring pain into your life. Don't fall for it. Recognize that mistakes will be made and lessons will be learned.

Dealing with behavior that runs counter to your Victor-Six without grace and mercy is not an option. Treat yourself or your spouse with love and understanding and you can quickly move beyond the trap. Blow up, beat yourself up, and generally act like a bully, and you will remain mired in the financial mess. This is a time to rise up and be the leader that you are, this is the time to prove you are Battle Ready.

After every encounter with the enemy on the battlefield, when the fighting is over and the troops have secured their positions, the field commanders, platoon leaders, and squad leaders, pull aside for an After Action Review. The purpose is not to lay blame, not to bring praise, but to simply understand what occurred, what went right, and what areas need to be improved.

During the AAR, each leader gives their assessment of what happened as viewed from their vantage point. They cover the actions they and their troops took, the outcome of those actions, and the current state of their squad. The other leaders listen, provide feedback, and make observations based on their own experiences in battle. Notes are made, lessons are learned, and they move on. Whatever mistakes were made are corrected and the leaders leave the meeting with a better understanding of how they need to react should a similar situation arise.

In a similar way, you should conduct your own After Action Review when you have had an encounter with the enemy. When mistakes have been made, take the time to examine what happened, take note of the lessons that are to be learned, and determine how to react the next time the situation arises. Rest assured if something caused you or your spouse to get off track once, you will face it again, probably more than once. That is how the enemy operates. The sooner you learn constructive ways to deal with having fallen into the trap, the sooner you will find the traps are no longer effective.

There are two key points to this ROE you need to make sure you understand. **The first is grace**. Extend grace, which is undeserved favor, to the person who made the mistake, even if it's you. Doing so will confuse the enemy, encourage the one who made the mistake, and strengthen their resolve to avoid the same behavior in the future.

The second key is to learn the lesson. There is value in messing up, but only if you take the time to see it. If you react by ranting and raving and do not examine the cause of the failure, you are destined to repeat the mistake over and over. If you keep your emotions in check and take a hard look at why the mistake was made, chances are, it will not be made again.

ROE # 5

Develop a plan to deal with impulse buying and snap decisions.

I once had a Tactical Officer who was fond of saying "Make a decision, even if it's wrong." While this does keep a young lieutenant from freezing up under pressure and losing valuable time on the battlefield, it can also lead to fatal mistakes. As long as those mistakes are made in training, corrected, and learned from, all is well.

However, if the first time a battlefield commander makes a mistake is in the heat of battle, bad things tend to happen. Snap decisions and impulse actions must be practiced and honed in a safe environment before they can be trusted. The cost is too high to make those mistakes when facing the enemy.

The same principals hold true for snap financial decisions.

If you have ever walked into a store with the intention of buying a few small items and walked out with a shopping cart full, you have experienced impulse buying. Manufacturers and retailers are very skilled in developing products that will cause you to believe you must have them right now.

Millions if not billions of dollars are spent on product design, testing, packaging, and shelf position in order to determine exactly what it takes to best separate you from your money. They know the colors that attract you, the words that cause you to act, and where in the store the display should be located so that you will put the item in your shopping cart. Selling is their profession and they are very good.

The evidence can usually be found in closets, garages, and attics. Take a look and see if you have anything stored away that you bought because you could not live without it. It could be exercise equipment that promises to give you rock hard abs in just 5 minutes a day, the latest and greatest tool for keeping your yard finely manicured, or a host of other "must have" items. Whatever it is, we have all fallen victim.

The first step in dealing with impulse buying is to become aware of your triggers. Take a look at the marketing that causes you to react. Merely becoming aware of what is happening can be enough to allow some people to deny the impulse. For others, awareness is a good first step, but they must go further.

Once you become aware of your triggers, take one of the following actions:

- Choose to avoid the types of stores that cause you to engage in impulse buying.

- Use a shopping list and stick to it.

- Only take enough money to pay for the things on your shopping list.

Since marketing is all around us, avoiding stores may not be practical. If you cannot avoid the store, you must take steps to avoid the behavior.

To stick to a shopping list, first make out a list of the item or items you need before you enter the store, only buy those items, and nothing more. If it's not on the list it does not get into the cart.

In a cash system taking only enough money to pay for the things that are on your shopping list is very effective. While you may give in to the impulse to put the item in the cart, there will be no money to buy it when you get to the register. Do this a few times and your desire to avoid embarrassment at the checkout counter will soon override your desire to buy things on impulse.

ROE # 6

Determine how you will deal with the unexpected.

When preparing for battle, it is often said it is better to have it and not need it than to need it and not have it. Read that again if you need to, it's okay. In the heat of the moment, when things are not going as you planned, having the resources available to help get you back on track is always preferable to not having the resources.

On long road marches, soldiers are always told to pack extra socks. In basic training, the drill instructors constantly harp on extra socks. As a young private who had never marched 20 miles before, I had no idea why I was to be worried about extra socks. It seemed to me I might want to pack extra food, maybe some reading material, a comfortable pillow, and some cash just in case we happened to march by a Burger King.

Though I questioned the need, I went ahead and packed several pairs of extra socks. I ended up having no room for a pillow which as it turned out was fine since sleeping was not really on the agenda, nor was reading, nor Burger King. We were in hard core, can't sleep, no time to read, got to get to the next check point training mode and the only thing that mattered was that we kept moving.

Around mile seven, a cool refreshing rain started falling. Slow at first, but steady. By mile eight, it was a full on downpour. Every stitch of clothing was wet and our boots were soaked through. While you may have never had the pleasure of wearing military issue olive drab green wool socks and black leather combat boots, while carrying a 60 pound ruck sack marching down a gravel road, on a steamy July night, on a base in Oklahoma, you can imagine our condition. We were tired, we were wet, our backs ached, and our feet hurt.

No one was thinking about reading, Burger King, or sleeping on a comfortable bed with a comfortable pillow. All we wanted was for the pain and discomfort to go away.

When the rain stopped, the wisdom of having those extra socks became self-evident. Wet wool surrounded by stiff leather compacted by a heavy load exerts a tremendous amount of pressure and friction on one's feet. As the skin becomes softened from hours of sweat and rain, the friction starts to takes a toll. The only solution is to have dry feet. The only way to have dry feet while walking through the rain is to have really good boots or several changes of socks. Since really good boots were not an option, extra socks saved the day. Every few hours, the march was stopped and everyone changed their socks. Feet were allowed to dry a bit, soggy socks were replaced with clean dry socks, and the mission continued.

In your mission to accomplish the outcome you desire, there will be a time when the rain starts to fall, when the load gets too heavy, and when you begin to ache from the task. The only question is will you be prepared? Will you have extra socks?

Extra socks could take on many forms in your mission. Extra cash in your wallet, extra money in your savings account, an emergency fund, or a buffer kept in your checking account are a few of the options. A low limit, low interest credit card, a personal line of credit, or a home equity line of credit could also be considered.

Much depends on your level of financial discipline and your circumstances. Whatever you decide, make sure that it is an actual solution to an actual problem and not an excuse to spend to make yourself feel better. More on this topic will be covered in the chapter called Battle Ready Budgets.

ROE # 7

Decide how you will reward yourself for hitting benchmarks.

Just as soldiers on the battlefield need time to pull away from the fight and enjoy a bit of R&R between missions, you also need to plan for rest and relaxation. Financial wars can be intense and care must be taken to always remember who the fight is with and why you are fighting. One of the best ways to accomplish this is to set up a system of rewards that will allow you to feel normal for a while, remind you of what life off the battlefield is like, and recharge your batteries for the next engagement.

Soldiers carry a map of the battlefield with mission objectives marked along the way and you too should carry a financial map. You should know where you are at all times so that when an objective is reached, you can dig in, reinforce your resolve, relax, and recharge.

Fighting for your finances with your spouse at your side can be stressful. You must avoid the trap of allowing that stress to cause you to turn on one another. Constantly denying yourself time to relax, to forget about money, and to just enjoy one another can be a major source of demotivation. Adding small rewards to the mix can help.

If you have a goal to pay off or pay down a debt, think of ways to reward the behavior along the way. Set benchmarks to mark your progress and celebrate as each benchmark is met. The celebrations do not need to be extravagant, just something that refreshes you and keeps you connected to your Victor-Six.

Maybe you have decided that you will stop eating out until you have reduced your debt by $1000. When the benchmark is hit, celebrate the victory with an affordable meal at a comfortable restaurant. Don't go crazy and add to your debt, but do have a date and celebrate the progress. Doing so allows you to acknowledge the sacrifice that has been made and reminds you that the pain is worth the result.

Perhaps you love to read but have decided to stop spending money on books until you have your budget under control. This is a good and worthy goal. Just don't get so intense and focused on the goal that you forget the person who is fighting toward its achievement. Find ways to feed your love of reading as you make progress with your budget. Allow yourself to go to the used bookstore, the library, or to purchase a low cost digital book whenever you reach an objective. While this may seem like a small thing, it is critical that you pull back from the fight from time to time.

This ROE is crucial for married couples as well as individuals. Financial stress can cause couples to turn on one another faster than almost anything else and cause individuals to turn on themselves. Remind yourself that the battle is not with your spouse and not with you by taking time to celebrate accomplishments that move you closer to your goal. This will relieve tension, reduce arguments, and promote better financial decisions in the future.

Acknowledge the struggle and reward the behavior that helped you reach the objective to keep your spirits high, your motivation strong, and drive you on to complete the mission.

ROE # 8

Don't try to be John Wayne.

"Everyone's a hero until the first shot is fired" is a phrase you often hear around our fighting men. Soldiers know that it's easy to talk a good game, but when bullets start flying, keeping your courage in the face of danger can be difficult. While most people want to be the hero who never backs down and always wins the day, you never really know for certain how you will react until you are in the middle of the fray. Often times, the ones who are the most vocal about what they are going to do are the very ones who shrink back and allow someone else to take the lead. Self-awareness is the key. Understand your fears, where you are weak, and seek help. There is no shame in asking for help.

In your financial fight, there will be times when you are overwhelmed. A common mistake is to act like you have it all under control, pretend that you are not afraid, and charge into the battle unprepared for what lies ahead. Your money is an intensely personal topic and you may be reluctant to talk about your mistakes. Because our society equates success with money, you may be embarrassed about your situation. You may be afraid of what someone will think if you open up and ask for help. If you find yourself in this position and feel it is better to risk more mistakes and more financial injury than having to suffer the discomfort of asking a professional for help, take a moment and think.

Think about the worst thing that can happen if you continue to play the hero and make bad financial decisions. Let that play out in your mind. First, your debts get out of control and you can't make the minimum payments. You fall behind on your car payments, your house payments, and your utility bills. Creditors begin to call around the clock. Stress and tension permeate your relationships and worry rules your mind. The bank comes and takes the car, the power company shuts off the power, and foreclosure proceedings are started on your home. Your pride has been your downfall. *"Where there is strife, there is pride, but wisdom is found in those who take advice."* Proverbs 13:10

Now, think about the best thing that could happen by seeking professional advice. Before you make your next big purchase plunging you further in debt, you decide to visit a Financial Planner. In the meeting you are brutally honest. It makes you uncomfortable to admit your mistakes, but you press on. Together with your spouse, you and the Financial Planner determine that making the purchase is not wise at this time. You map out a plan of action to pay down some debt. You set a timeline for when the purchase can be made and begin saving toward the goal. You begin to understand the process known as the "Debt Snowball" and you start to envision a day when your debts are paid off. It looks a lot like freedom.

Those few moments of being uncomfortable, embarrassed, and afraid of what someone might think are a small price to pay for peace of mind. Regardless of your situation, you don't have to be John Wayne. You don't have to rescue the damsel in distress on your own. Find a professional partner, develop a plan, and get to work. There will be heavy lifting involved, but you are up to the challenge. You are becoming Battle Ready.

ROE # 9

Decide to put the first things first.

In every conflict, armed or otherwise, there are critical elements that must be addressed if the mission is to be successful. On the battlefield, missing these elements will greatly reduce the fighting force's ability to wage war. Usually, these items are simple routine things that must be dealt with first. It is important to keep the first things first.

One of the first and most critical things is troop health. Health and Welfare Inspections are conducted weekly if not more. Physical and emotional health must be a top priority to maintain force strength. Proper hygiene, handling and storage of rations, maintaining clean drinking water, and the proper care of wounds are essential. Something as simple as dysentery can cripple an entire platoon of hardened soldiers.

As important as physical health is, emotional and mental health are just as crucial. Allowing a squad, platoon, company, or battalion to become infected with the disease of apathy toward the cause will be devastating to the outcome and safety of the men. A good commander must be able to recognize and replace destructive emotions before they spread among the men and women in uniform. Troop morale must be maintained.

To do so, commanders continually relay the Victor-Six-Vision. It must be on their lips at all times. The Victor-Six ensures that all decisions made on the ground are in support of the mission and does not allow bad attitudes and sour opinions to poison the entire group. When all involved can clearly understand the Victor-Six, clearly communicate the desired outcomes, and fully understand their role in the mission, keeping the first things first follows naturally.

In your mission to square away your finances, you must also keep your first things first. You should strive to maintain a positive mental attitude, good physical condition, and keep your Victor-Six on your lips at all times. You must understand that when your emotions begin to fight against your vision and your health begins to wane, you open an opportunity for the enemy to strike, and strike he will.

Your enemy knows you well. He has observed you in action all of your life. He knows what makes you angry, what makes you sad, and what causes you to lose hope. He will stop at nothing to defeat you and using your over stressed emotions and weak physical condition to make you doubt your resolve and quit is a classic strategy. **The first things to be aware of are these: Stay aware of your attitudes, your thoughts, your feelings, and those of your spouse. If you see cracks begin to form in one of these areas, take whatever steps you need to reinforce your defenses.**

There is nothing wrong with taking a break from the action. When the struggle becomes so intense that you begin to snap at one another, it could be a sign that a short respite from the fight is in order. Pull back, celebrate your progress and regroup. Above all else, do not allow yourself to arrive at the place where apathy about your mission begins to set in. Keep the first things first and you will soon have the enemy on the run.

ROE # 10

Never underestimate the resourcefulness of the enemy.

In combat, a healthy respect for the capabilities of your enemy is always in order. Notice I did not say to respect your enemy, only what he is capable of doing. You should loathe your enemy. You need to understand that his goal is your total destruction. He has no mercy, no sense of fair play, and will not relent until he is forced to do so. He will lie to you, trick you, and use your best friends against you if possible.

As soldiers in this battle, you must be *"wise as serpents and innocent as doves"* Matt 10:16.

Wise as serpents so that you will recognize the attacks and from where they come. Innocent as doves in order to continue to walk in love toward those who are unwittingly used against you by your enemy. When you understand this principal, you will begin to see that indeed *"you are not fighting against flesh-and-blood enemies, but against evil rulers and authorities of the unseen world, against mighty powers in this dark world, and against evil spirits in the heavenly places."* Eph 6:12.

In other words, your fight is not with your spouse, it is not with the people at the credit card company, the bank, or the collection agency. Your battle is against the darkness of this world and its embedded system of power and control. Recognition of this fact will allow you to focus on the true nature of your enemy.

If you find this idea unsettling, take courage. *"You have already won a victory over those people, because the Spirit who lives in you is greater than the spirit who lives in the world. Those people belong to this world, so they speak from the world's viewpoint, and the world listens to them. But we belong to God, and those who know God listen to us. If they do not belong to God, they do not listen to us. That is how we know if someone has the Spirit of truth or the spirit of deception."* 1 John 4:4-6

The enemy is beaten, the victory is won through the work of Christ on the cross, and you now must walk in that victory. Understand who the enemy is, get to know his tactics, but do not fear him. Determine to see your mission through to your desired outcome and partner with God to make it happen. Engage in the battle knowing the victory will be yours. This is the essential mindset of the Battle Ready Financial Warrior.

Battle Ready Training Task 2.1

Determine Your Rules of Engagement

In this chapter, you have learned the importance of Rules of Engagement. You have become aware of the need to eliminate guesswork during combat. You now understand that making the same decisions over and over is ineffective and inefficient. In order to coordinate the actions of your force, ROE must be established before facing the enemy.

Time to take action: This is your fight. As the battlefield commander, you get to make the rules. With your Victor-Six-Vision as your guide, develop as many rules as you feel necessary in order to facilitate the battle. Remember, the goal of Rules of Engagement is to make as many decisions as possible ahead of time in order to eliminate confusion, reduce battlefield stress, and provide continuity of action among all who are involved.

You may decide to have two rules or you may decide you need many more. You may decide to use the ten rules given as examples or you may be completely original. The key is to get started, anticipate as many possible areas of ambiguity as you can, and develop a set of ROE to address them.

Set aside one hour, more if needed, and decide on at least 5 ROE dealing with the following areas:

Spending Limits

-How much per person per day?

-How much without talking to your spouse first?

-How long is your cooling off period?

Method of Daily Operation

-Cash, debit card, or checks?

Common Areas of Attack

-What items, hobbies, or wants cause you to spend the most?

-When there is financial tension, how will you deal with it?

Rewards for Achieving Benchmarks

-As targets are reached, how will you celebrate?

-What will you do to build morale?

-What are the most effective ways to encourage your fellow troops?

Physical and Emotional Health

-What will you do to stay strong in the face of battle?

-When you recognize negative emotions, how will you help resolve them?

-Should a break from the action be required, how long before the fighting resumes?

Along with your Victor-Six, the Rules of Engagement build a foundation on which your Battle Ready Financial Plan will stand. Without these two elements firmly in place, clearly communicated, accepted and understood by all involved, and ingrained in your thinking, you will suffer ongoing wounds. Get these two elements right, and they will propel you to new heights in your financial fight, allowing you to reach targets that may have once seemed unattainable. Do not move forward until this foundation is laid. Your financial future depends on it.

Chapter 3

Build a Battle Ready Budget

"For which of you, wanting to build a tower, doesn't first sit down and calculate the cost to see if he has enough to complete it?" Luke 14:28

Now we get to the nitty-gritty. Budgeting is where the rubber meets the road. While you may find the idea of budgeting to be boring, it is important that you hang in there for this part of the training. **You are going to learn a method of budgeting that you have likely never seen before.** Battle Ready Budgeting is a new way to handle your finances that will give you confidence, freedom, and soon have you on the right track. Lace up those boots and get ready for a bit of hard core financial training.

It's no secret that Uncle Sam has a spending problem. While it may seem a bit foolish to look to the Department of Defense for a lesson on how to live within your means, there are things that can be learned.

Financially speaking, our government is the worst offender. Each year budget deficits are the norm and an ever expanding national debt is the result. There will come a day when all those trillions of debt must be dealt with, which is another reason your finances need to be in top condition. Taking steps now to put your own financial house in order will place you in the best position to weather the storm should the nation's financial house begin to crumble.

Military units function on directives known as Operations Orders. This written document begins at the highest level of command and describes the overall mission. A good Operations Order lists the units available to put into action, determines how and where each of those units will be used, outlines objectives for each unit, and describes the risks involved.

The order then goes down to the next level commanders. Those leaders go through the Operations Order taking the information they need to complete their part of the mission and write an Operations Order for those in their command. This process is repeated until every division, brigade, battalion, company, and platoon has received instructions and know exactly what their role in the conflict will be. The Operations Order keeps the urge to micro manage at bay and allows each unit to complete their part of the mission. This allows leaders to focus on their area of concern knowing that all other supporting units are doing their part.

In effect, the Operations Order is the written plan of every action required to ensure the mission is successful. It takes into account all resources available and then allows each unit commander to determine how to best use those resources to complete their mission tasks.

The Operations Order allows for the efficient use of resources, eliminates repetitive decision making, and identifies weak areas that need to be addressed. It clearly determines when and where each asset will be deployed and removes all confusion about what actions are to be taken. All decisions that can be made ahead of time are made before the battle begins allowing for quick action when the time comes.

The ideal result is a lean efficient fighting force that knows exactly what to expect and is prepared to take action when the time comes. This process is very similar to making financial decisions that support the mission and is a good model from which to build our own Battle Ready Budget.

The modern budget has been adapted from a device originally created by government bean counters. The goal was to determine how little each employee could be paid and still maintain a minimum standard of living, not as a method to operate a family spending plan.

We have taken a concept intended to prescribe how much a government employee ought to be paid and turned it into the only acceptable method of how one should account for their monthly spending. The result is a repetitive, labor intensive exercise in futility.

Budgeting the way you have learned in the past is inefficient and ineffective.

While a traditional household budget may seem like a good tool to help you manage your money, the reality is that the old way of budgeting adds to your stress, while doing little to solve your money woes.

The old budget asks you to remake the same decisions every month, to be ever mindful of every penny spent, and to keep detailed records of the same events over and over and over.

While knowing what you earn and spend is necessary, knowing it over and over again is not. Once you have established what needs to be accomplished, determined the assets available, and committed the assets to a particular task, stop stressing and move on to other pursuits.

All families, all people, and all companies follow patterns. We each have things that we do exactly the same way every time. We have developed habits that cause us to take the same course of action over and over again. Though some habits can be destructive, we can use this tendency of repetitive actions to automate our budget process and eliminate repetitive decision making. While you may face new challenges every day, there are certain elements regarding your money that are the same month in and month out, year after year. It is in these areas that major strides in efficiency and effectiveness can be made with very little effort.

Imagine a small fighting force of 12 men called 1st Squad. Each member is given detailed written instructions on what is expected of them: how to take up a fighting position, how to load their weapon, how to aim for best results, and when to fire at the enemy. The men are then sent immediately to the front lines. There is no training beforehand, and the soldiers must keep the written document to consult each time they do the next task or make a routine decision.

Before they dig a fox hole, they need to read to see how deep to make it. Before they load their weapon, they need to check the specs and see how much ammo it will hold. Before taking aim, they need to see how the rear and front sights work together. Every task, every decision, every course of action requires each soldier to check the manual.

Now picture this unit being ordered to consult the manual every time, giving no thought to how they performed the task the last time. How efficient would a unit like this be? How long would they survive in battle?

Imagine the frustration of the squad leader as he tries to ensure all twelve men are doing what they are supposed to do, what they have been given detailed instructions on how to do. Though the battle is raging on, every time someone needs to reload, he has to stop and consult the manual for the number of shells to use. This untrained, low functioning unit would be wiped out in a matter of hours.

Were that scene to be played out in combat, the troops that survived the first battle would soon realize that in order to remain among the living, they are going to have to improvise. They will need to think on their feet, tackle tasks as they come up, and accomplish them to the best of their ability any way they can, regardless of what the manual says. Toss the instructions, react to the battle, and live to fight another day.

As ridiculous as that scenario is, **it's a pretty accurate description of how a traditional budget operates, detailing month after month or week after week how to do the same tasks that you did the month or week before.** Nothing spent without first checking the budget. No decision made without first running the numbers. Though your house payment is always the same, you still must write down how much will be spent on the house each month, determine when to send the money in, and then go through the exercise of writing the check and dropping it in the mail. Every month, year after year after year.

Let's learn and put to use a better, more efficient way to fight your financial battle.

Modern warfare is fast and furious. There is no time to consult a field manual in the heat of battle. Troops must be sufficiently trained and fully capable to complete the mission. We called it being "high speed and low drag". Soldiers strive to find the most efficient way to complete the task while eliminating unnecessary actions.

Go back to the battlefield and imagine another small squad of troops called 2nd Squad. They are continually engaged in fighting and are doing the best they can to stay alive. There are 12 men; each highly trained to perform his job within the squad and one squad leader making decisions. Before the conflict ever begins, each squad member is highly trained.

In the heat of battle, no one has to consult with the squad leader during the fight and no one needs the manual. Each soldier performs to their highest capability and the squad functions as a finely tuned machine. Because of the work that took place in training, they are battle ready before ever facing the enemy. They know their jobs, they work together, and they accomplish the mission.

This type of unit will have success. They will have trained together and will know their own capabilities as well as those around them. They will know the strengths and weaknesses of each member of the squad. They will understand the units Victor-Six and will know the Rules of Engagement. All the decisions that can be made before the conflict begins will have been made. The result is an unburdened, unencumbered, and highly effective fighting force, the exact type of force you want in place when the stuff starts to hit the fan.

Financially speaking, the old way of budgeting can get you killed. Just like our 1st Squad, it can leave you guessing what to do next, digging for the filed manual in the heat of battle, remaking decisions that should already have been made.

Once you go through the work and frustration of completing the old type budget a few times, one of two things will happen. You will either love the budget and find it works perfect for you or you will toss it out claiming budgeting does not work.

Statistics suggest that many more people get frustrated and toss out budgeting than those who embrace budgeting.

If you have tried and failed at the old way of budgeting, there is good news. Battle Ready Budgeting and the BRB Tool will ease your frustration, reduce repetitive decisions, and focus your attention where it is needed most.

The old budget falls short in the real world. Though it may be a good written plan, when the flaming arrows start flying, traditional budgets cannot adjust. **You end the month with a written plan that serves to point out all the ways you messed up.**

When the financial battle begins, even the best plans can fall to the wayside as the bills come in. A mistimed expenditure, a delay in receiving a paycheck, or a miscalculation in the timing of cash flow, and the budget is blown.

To compensate, you must sort through all categories to find resources to cover the shortfall. The most common course of action after this has occurred for the second or third time is to give up and believe budgets are useless and you just can't make it work. Toss the instructions and react to the battle.

Therein lies the problem. It is not really that traditional budgeting techniques don't work, just that they take more discipline than most people have and cause more frustration than most people want to deal with. As a result, they scrap the budget and go back to their old habits.

Call it the "Hassle Factor." When it becomes more of a hassle to work out a budget than the apparent rewards it brings, the budget gets eighty-sixed and the improvising begins.

American author William Feather once wrote "A budget tells us what we can't afford, but it does not stop us from buying it." A budget is nothing more than a combat manual: a guide that can work well in an ideal environment and is only as flexible as the one who develops it allows.

Good budgets have contingencies built in for common occurrences and set funds aside to take care of those need. A good budget is a tool you can use to plan your attack.

While good is okay, in the fight for your finances, you need to be better than good. You need to do more than plan the attack. You need to execute the plan, adjust as needed, and know every step of the way the resources you have to employ. You need to be Battle Ready.

Unit Development

Donald Rumsfeld, the 21st US Secretary of Defense once said "There are things we know that we know. There are also known unknowns. That is to say there are things that we now know we don't know. But there are also unknown unknowns. There are things we do not know we don't know. So when we do the best we can and we pull all this information together, and we then say well that's basically what we see as the situation, that is really only the known knowns and the known unknowns. And each year, we discover a few more of those unknown unknowns."

Go back and read that a few more times if you need to. I'll wait.

What at first glance appears to be a riddle or a crafty bit of political speak, is actually a very astute observation and the perfect framework on which to base our Battle Ready Budget.

There are things we know that we know. For instance, we know that every month, our house payment will come due for the same amount on the same day of the month. We know for sure it will happen until the day we make the last payment. It is a known known. These known knowns provide an excellent opportunity to improve our method of budgeting and make efficient use of our resources.

Then, there are things that we know that we don't know. We don't know if our utility bill is going to be $200 or $250 but we know that we will have to pay something. We don't know if our groceries will cost $375 or $475 but we know that we will have to eat. We don't know how much it will cost to put gas in our car this month but we know we will need to go places in the car. We know that we don't know exactly what these costs are going to be. These are known unknowns. These known unknowns are our daily living expenses. These are the things we need to pay close attention to.

Then, there are those things that we don't know that we don't know. We don't know the air conditioner is going to stop working in the middle of July. We don't know our car is going to die on the interstate requiring a tow to the mechanic. We don't know the flu is going to run through our family increasing medical bills and causing us to miss work. These are things we can't predict. These are unknown unknowns. Because the possibility these things may occur is very real, we must take steps to be prepared. Though we don't know what may occur or when it may happen, we can be sure that there will be times in our lives unexpected things requiring money to correct them will happen.

When applied to our budget, these three categories can be called Fixed Expenses, Household Expenses, and Emergency Expenses.

The old way of budgeting would have these categories lumped together in one place, each a line item that must be detailed every month. Using the old method, you break down each of those expenses into individual dollar amounts and write them on your sheet of paper. Every month. Go into great detail and ensure that you never go over, watching every penny as it goes to its assigned task.

Never mind that the house payment is always the same, write it down. Never mind that the car payment never changes, write it down. Make the same decision every month. Fill the same envelope with the same amount of money every month and then take it out every month at the same time to pay the same bill. Month after month after month. The old way of budgeting has you ever mindful of all of those fixed expenses that never change until something is paid off. Put the money in, take the money out, put the money in and you shake it all about. Do the hokey pokey and turn yourself around, that's what it's all about. A waste of time and effort.

In the Battle Ready Budget, any decision that is repeated every month needs only be made once. Figure out what you need to do, set it to repeat, and then forget about it. Write the Operations Order to ensure the need is met but don't micro-manage. Do the heavy lifting one time then put it on auto pilot. This new way of budgeting will help you become lean and efficient in your money management and thought process.

The Battle Ready Budget has three goals:

- **Efficient Use of Resources to ensure all your bills are paid on time.**

- **Elimination of Repetitive Decision Making by separating your expenses, moving those that**

repeat into a designated account and automating where possible.

- **Identification of Weaknesses or Deficiencies in the plan by developing an accurate method to track the resources and prepare for the unexpected.**

This new way of budgeting dictates that you change your thinking about money. Instead of considering everything you spend money on as one big group called something like expenses or outflow, the Battle Ready Budget draws some distinctions.

Recurring monthly expenses are referred to as "bills". These are fixed known expenses for which someone or some company sends a request for payment to you every month. Your "bills" are things that must be paid or bad things start to happen. When the bills go unpaid, collectors start calling and your stress builds. Do this long enough and angry looking men may come and start taking your stuff away. At some point, they may ask you to leave your home. When the bills go unpaid, life is just not good. Most of your bills will fall into your Fixed Expense category.

There are also those things you spend money for every month for which no one sends an invoice. These are things you go out and intentionally purchase. These are your Household Expenses and include things like food, toiletries, dining out, gas for your car, etc. These are expenditures that you have direct control over and things that can be reduced or eliminated without causing major ramifications with a bank or a third party. These are your true "expenses". Expenses may also occur monthly but they do not involve a request for payment.

While this distinction is not always clear, it is helpful to begin thinking in these terms as we move forward with the Battle Ready Budget.

In addition, there are those bills that occur one time and cannot always be predicted. These could include a bill for an unexpected doctor visit, a bill for a repair to a vehicle, or a bill to cover the cost of a home repair. These one-time unexpected bills will go into the Emergency Expense category. Because these things are not known ahead of time and cannot always be anticipated, they need to be treated separately. Spending for these type items are referred to as simply Emergency Expenses. In the Battle Ready Budget, money is set aside each month to take care of the Emergency Expenses as they arise.

With an understanding of the differences between bills, expenses, and Emergency Expenses in place, the three goals of the BRB can be better understood. The first goal is to ensure all your "bills" are paid on time and are automated. Setting your budget up to make sure that all of your fixed expenses are paid before you spend money on things you have direct control over keeps you in good standing with the people whom you owe money. This keeps your credit healthy, your bankers happy, and eliminates a large amount of stress.

The second goal is separation. Moving fixed recurring bills into a different account helps you to see what your essential obligations truly are. With a clear understanding of the amounts needed for your bills each month, you are in a position to set automatic payments to occur ensuring goal number one is met.

This Separation and Automation allows you to then shift your focus to the only area of your budget in which you actually have control, your Household spending.

When you separate and automate your deposits and withdrawals in a way that your bills are met and the payments go out on auto pilot, you eliminate the possibility of spending money you do not have. This separation keeps you on track, forces you to handle your money in the right way, and causes you to live within your means.

The third goal is to understand what you really have to spend. This is an outflow of the first two goals. When you learn the BRB method, you will have determined the amount needed to cover your monthly bills, have set up your income to be deposited, and have the bills set to be automatically paid.

When this is done properly, you get a clear understanding of how much you really have to take care of your expenses each month. You will know without a doubt how much you can spend on your Household expenses and how much you can set aside for the Emergency Expenses that may come up. You won't have to guess, you won't have to recalculate each month, and you won't have to play it by ear. You will know, and knowing is half the battle.

A budget that can accomplish these three goals on an ongoing basis will reduce your money induced stress, empower you to make better financial decisions based on

more accurate information, and increase your money communication in all of your relationships.

What components are needed to operate a successful Battle Ready Budget? To see the answer, look at how our nation's military is structured.

In a typical military unit there are several types of troops. There are Infantry who do the day to day grunt work. There are Airborne who are smaller, leaner forces able to support the action wherever they are needed and drop in at a moment's notice. The Cavalry, used primarily for reconnaissance and security, are mounted troops who in pop culture tend to ride in at the last moment and save the day. Finally, there are Reserve Units, who are used on an as needed basis for support in all areas. While there are other types of units, these four fit nicely into our Battle Ready Budget Plan.

In your Battle Ready Budget, you need four things: An Infantry Unit (Fixed Expenses), an Airborne Unit (Household Expenses), a Cavalry Unit (Emergency Expenses), and a Reserve Unit (Savings).

As the battlefield commander, it is your job to see that all four units are fully equipped to carry out their mission. You are responsible for oversight, command and control, and resupply orders. You write the Operations Order and then allow the units to carry out their orders and complete the mission each month.

The Infantry Unit

In every fighting force, the troops on the ground are key to establishing authority and control on the battlefield. While modern war may be waged from the air, it is not until the infantry arrives to take over the area that peace can begin to be established.

The same can be said for your Battle Ready Budget. Until you have a properly set up and funded Infantry Unit, peace in your finances will be hard to come by.

Your Infantry will take care of all of your known bills or Fixed Expenses every month. It handles the grunt work of monthly slogging through all your fixed monthly payments.

This unit handles your car payment, house payment, insurance payment, debt payment, and all other bills that recur on a monthly basis in the same amount. It should include your tithes, cable, cellphone, internet, and pest control. Everything that happens each month in the same amount at the same time gets assigned to this unit. If you get a bill in the mail, the Infantry Unit portion of your BRB takes care of it. If you send the same amount to the same organization every month, the Infantry Unit is the place to channel the resources needed.

Once all items have been assigned to the Infantry, total the amounts. Ensure the required amount of money is allocated to meet all of its obligations and deposited into the account using the Battle Ready Budget Calendar. Total once and resupply every month at the appropriate times. Set both the income and the expenditures to happen on auto pilot and you will stay mentally uncluttered. It will allow the Infantry to do the job you have given them while you turn your attention elsewhere.

You can sleep well knowing that as long as you give them the supplies they need (the income necessary to meet your fixed expenses) the Infantry will get the job done.

I know for some of you, this flies in the face of your thinking. Somewhere in your past, a well-meaning guru may have beaten into you the idea that you must know where every dollar is going and assign it a job to do before you ever earn the dollar. You need to know in absolute detail where your resources are going. Without doing this, you will fail, plain and simple.

If that is coming up for you right now, you can relax. Once you understand this process, you will see that you will know exactly what is happening with your finances.

In the Infantry Unit (Fixed Expenses), you do know what the money is doing. You know it is taking care of everything that needs to be taken care of, every month.

It is not necessary for you to know, that is to think about, contemplate, worry about, and stress over the details. Knowing all this --> $750 is paying your house payment, $65 goes to your cable, $273 takes care of the car, $600 for your tithe, $500 for debt service, $70 knocks out the home insurance, $45 for the car insurance, $25 for the life insurance, your cell phones are $285, your home internet is $50, and your home phone is $25 <-- is not necessary.

Once you have arrived at the totals, know when the money needs to be in the account, and have it automated, it is enough to know that the Infantry gets $2,688 every month.

You can sleep well at night knowing that the Infantry has you covered.

You will need to work out the amounts and coordinate the timing of the paycheck or the income allocation for each week. After that, if you have consistent income, your only responsibility is to ensure a sufficient amount of resources are allocated to the Infantry Unit to meet its ongoing obligations and have those resources deposited in a timely manner.

The Battle Ready Budgeting spreadsheet will give you the necessary tools to make this happen and can be downloaded for free at www.BattleReadyFinance.com.

For those whose income changes with each paycheck, the BRB will help you see exactly how much you need to earn to pay your bills. You will know if you need to work an extra shift, take on a side job, or put in some overtime. You will know to the penny how much you have to come up with and when you need it. You won't have to wonder, you will know.

To work out the coordination of income dates and fixed expense dates, use the Battle Ready Budget Tool located at www.BattleReadyFinance.com.

This method leaves you one amount to track, a dozen bills to "forget" about, and peace of mind knowing that your essential fixed costs are taken care of, regardless of what happens the rest of the month.

Budgeting this way ensures your fixed expenses are dealt with and you never miss a payment. Add automatic deposits and automatic payments to your Infantry and simplify your finances even further.

An Infantry Unit on auto pilot is the first part of a highly efficient Battle Ready Budget.

The Airborne Unit

Having taken care of the known knowns, it is time to look at the known unknowns.

Those things that you know you will spend money on; you are just not sure how much. These are your Household Expenses and they will be taken care of by your Airborne Unit. This unit is smaller, more flexible, and can be used as necessary at the battlefield commander's discretion.

The Airborne Unit (Household Expense Account) is the most like traditional budgeting. You will track every withdrawal from this account and keep a running total. Staying aware of what is available in this account on any given day is critical. You will learn to track your spending and gain an understanding of exactly how much money you have to run your household. You will know the amount you can spend without impacting your Fixed Expenses, knowing that all of your bills have been paid by the money that is in the Infantry Unit.

In this unit, you will include funds for things such as food, gas, entertainment, clothing, toiletries, and any other expense that is not fixed. This account is for the things you use daily, the things you do for entertainment, and the things you buy out of necessity.

The amounts you allocate should be based on averages, with a buffer added as needed. This fund will require you to use sound judgment and will force communication between those using the money.

The Airborne Unit is your catch-all. It takes care of all of the things the Infantry does not handle. You will need debit card and check access to these funds and the ability to direct resources from this unit as needed.

The Airborne Unit (Household Expense Account) will require speed and flexibility. You may pull assets into the Airborne from the Cavalry Unit (Emergency Fund) should the need arise as well as deploy some of the Airborne resources back into the Cavalry at the end of the month. Managing your finances in this way changes your focus and allows you to use the resources you have in a much more efficient manner.

In a typical month, let's assume you spend an average of $400 on groceries and toiletries, $200 on gas, $150 on entertainment, and $50 on clothes. Add another $150 for dining out and fast food, $35 for school lunches, $100 for hobbies, and assume utilities run you $185. Your Airborne Unit should receive a minimum of $1270 plus a cushion of $100, for a total of $1,370.

That is all the money you have to spend.

If you bring home $5,300 a month, you still only get to spend what you have allocated to your Airborne Unit as the remainder will be used by the Infantry (Fixed Expenses), Cavalry (Emergency Expenses), and Reserve (Savings) Units to complete their missions. In a pinch, you can bring in the Cavalry, but you should strive to keep the Airborne a lean as possible. No overstaffing the Airborne to justify more resources. You are not a politician and this is not the DOD. These are your resources so make the most of them.

Everything that you buy on a daily basis that requires you to write a check, pay cash, or use a debit card will be purchased using money from the Airborne Unit.

While the goal for the Infantry Unit is full automation, the Airborne Unit is the opposite. **The income that goes into the Airborne Unit can be automated but the expenses should not be.**

Anything that you buy or spend money on by handing cash to a person, swiping a debit card in a machine, or writing a check to cover the cost will come out of this Household Expense Account.

Operating manually from this account keeps you aware of exactly how much is being spent and allows you to track the progress of the unit. This will require you and your spouse to talk about where the money is going and help you locate areas where resources are being wasted.

You cannot steal from your Infantry Unit or they will suffer a mission failure. Discipline yourself to only use the resources of the Airborne for your household needs.

With these two units, Infantry and Airborne, you will win a lot of financial battles while saving time and reducing stress.

The Cavalry Unit

One of the most basic financial lessons that many people miss is the establishment of an Emergency Fund. **Keeping money available to take care of unknown unknowns' is absolutely critical.**

Things happen, sometimes bad things. Often, these bad things are accompanied by the need for money. When there is no money available because you have neglected to establish an Emergency Fund, your only option is to take on debt. You will borrow money from family, friends, the bank, a credit card, or some other source to get you through the emergency.

A much better option is to set aside a little money from each paycheck so that when you are in a bind, you have the resources to take care of the need.

The Cavalry Unit is where the Emergency Fund is to be established.

No fighting force is complete without a well-staffed and trained Cavalry. These are the guys that provide security. They ride in and save the day. Just when you think your position is about to be overtaken, the Cavalry arrives to beat back the enemy and strengthen your position. This is a strong fighting force but you should not rely on the Cavalry for your day to day battle. Have them ready to deploy at a moment's notice, but keep them well rested and well fed if possible. Someday, when you least expect it, you may need to call on them to save your skin.

An ideal goal for your Cavalry Unit (Emergency Expenses) is enough resources to cover three to six months of fixed expenses that are normally handled by your Infantry Unit.

Start with five to ten percent from each paycheck and fund until complete. Using our numbers from above, funding you Cavalry Unit at $360 per month will build a month's worth of Infantry duties, or $2,688 every 7 1/2 months.

Should you suffer a job loss, you will have money available to continue to meet your monthly fixed expenses while you search for a new position. If you become ill and can no longer work, you will have the resources to provide for your needs while you recover. A well-funded Cavalry Unit just makes good sense.

Decide on the amount you will allocate to take care of the Emergency Expenses each month and have your bank set that money aside in a separate savings account. Automate this process and then forget the money is there.

While it may take some time to get there, completing this unit as soon as possible is critical to becoming Battle Ready.

The Reserve Unit

The fourth component of a Battle Ready Budget is the Reserve Unit (Savings). The Reserve Unit is the only unit that is allowed to get fat and happy. **The goal is that this unit will only be deployed at predetermined future dates but will also stand at the ready to assist other units as needed**.

The Reserve Unit should receive funding from every paycheck every time. Ten percent of your net pay is a good place to start, fifteen percent is better. **But, even one percent is better than nothing**. Adding $600 to $900 to your Reserve Unit will allow you to support the overall mission as necessary while still building resources for short term targets.

Perhaps you need to save for vehicle repairs. The Reserve Unit is the place to save. Perhaps you have a target to buy a home in five years. The Reserve Unit should hold the down payment. The Reserve Unit can be used for any expense that will come at some predetermined point in the future.

Building your Reserve Unit is a mission critical activity. Not only does the Reserve Unit hold the funds necessary to fund short term targets and see your long term dreams realized, but if the unthinkable happens and the Cavalry is depleted, you will want to have funds available to call up the Reserves.

Not only does setting money aside from each paycheck allow you to build a pool of resources for future purchases, it also helps to shape who you are. Instead of being a person who lives paycheck to paycheck never looking beyond today's bills, you begin to see things differently.

You begin to understand that you have more control, have more choices, and have more power over your life. You begin to have a sense of freedom that you never had when living hand to mouth knowing that if there is a need to be addressed, you can address it; if there is something God is calling you to do, you have the resources to do it.

In other words, you are building margin to take care of future dreams, goals, and missions.

Developing the habit of saving from every paycheck will make you feel less vulnerable to the attacks of the enemy.

When your Reserve Unit is established, you will have the peace of knowing that from a financial perspective, you are prepared for whatever comes your way. In other words, you will be Battle Ready.

Implementation

Do you see what's happening? Instead of dealing with a total income of $5,318 a month and detailing where every dollar is going, your Battle Ready Budget makes 80 – 90% of the decisions for you, removes the guesswork, and eliminates the stress of missing payments.

Once you have this process down, you only need to be concerned with the Airborne Unit and track the spending from that one account.

Everything else is set up to run on auto pilot. Just like a well written Operations Order, the BRB will empower you to focus on the things that will make the mission a success while allowing the things that can be taken care of by other units to proceed without your input. This keeps you lean, uncluttered, and focused.

The reality is that Battle Ready Budgeting is a simple and effective method of allocating your resources to accomplish the mission, which is guided by your Victor-Six and conforms to your personal Rules of Engagement.

The only thing left to determine is how to set up your four Units. A very effective method is to use four separate bank accounts.

The Infantry Unit (Fixed Expense Account) will receive the largest portion of income and will have the largest number of withdrawals that repeat on a monthly basis. Most of you have this account in place already. It should be a checking account **without** debit cards. No withdrawals outside of a fixed expense will be allowed from this account. These are mission critical items that must be handled every month. Repetitive grunt work is well suited for your Infantry unit. Funding this unit can occur through direct deposit from your employer or through directions given to your bank for each paycheck.

The Airborne Unit (Household Expense Account) will be a second, smaller checking account **with debit cards for each authorized member**. This is the account you will operate out of on a daily basis. If you need cash, it comes from this account. Spending money comes from this account. Fun money and mad money come from this account.

This is the only account you will need to balance and keep an eye on income and outflow. Once you have this concept down, maintaining this account will become a simple task that will allow you to understand areas in which you can cut expenses if needed, or splurge if possible. Again, funding can come through direct deposit or through standing instructions at the bank.

The Cavalry Unit (Emergency Expense Account) and the Reserve Unit (Savings Account) should be two distinct savings accounts both having the ability to transfer resources to the Airborne Unit as needed with either a phone call to the bank or through the bank website.

Four accounts set up, one account to maintain. Automation is the key. Automate your deposits to all four accounts. Enough to cover your fixed expenses to the Infantry, enough to cover your household expenses plus a cushion to the Airborne, enough to build your emergency fund to the Cavalry, and enough to meet your savings goals to the Reserves.

Automate your fixed payments and use the cash method or debit cards for your household expenditures. Simple, clean, and effective.

Battle Ready Budgeting will save you time, money, and heartache.

For help on determining how much income goes to each unit from each paycheck, use the BRB Tool located at www.battlereadyfinance.com.

Those with uncertain incomes will find this method of budgeting especially helpful.

By placing all of your fixed expenses into one account, you will know exactly how much to the penny you must earn in order cover critical items. This number will allow you to determine if you need to sell more, work more, provide more service, or do whatever it is you do to earn income. Knowing your fixed costs will ensure you never miss a payment and keep you motivated to bring home the bacon.

With your household expenses in the separate Airborne Unit, it is easier to find places to cut back when income falls short. Your fixed expenses are already taken care of and you know your spending from the household account will not interfere with the Infantry. If you begin to run short in the Airborne Unit, you can chose to spend less or pull from the Cavalry as needed. If you find that you have resources left in your Airborne Unit at the end of the month, that money can be moved into the Cavalry Unit to cover future emergencies or into the Reserve Unit to fund future purchases.

The key is that you are in control. No more wondering if you have the money to go out to dinner. No more fussing whether or not to spend money on things you want to buy.

The BRB method will keep you fully aware of your unit capabilities at all times. You will simply know that you do not have the money to in the household account to spend if that is the case.

You will know when the next paycheck is coming into the account and by using the Battle Ready Budgeting Tool; you will know the expenses that will be coming out. They say knowledge is power and if that is true, the BRB will give you more power over your finances than any other method.

The Battle Ready Budget provides the information you need to make wise decisions, stay true to your Victor-Six, and stay within your mission parameters.

Some reading this may feel that four accounts are not necessary. Combining the Calvary (Emergency Fund) and Reserves (Savings) into one Unit could work, but keeping them separate will serve you better as you move further into the Battle Ready Finance series. In later books, it will become more important to separate short term savings needs and long term objectives. Establishing all four accounts now will save you time in the future.

You may also choose to go old school and do everything manually. While I don't recommend it, you could use shoe boxes, envelopes, buckets, pots, bags, or any other container in place of bank accounts. The cash method might make sense for your household spending and could work for you, but the other three units will be more difficult to operate.

Each month you could cash your check. You could place the money needed for the Infantry (Fixed Expenses) into one shoe box, the Airborne (Household Expenses) into another, the Cavalry (Emergency Fund) into a third, and the Reserve (Savings) into a fourth. You could sub divide each unit into individual expenditures from each bucket of money and place it into separate envelopes. You could go into great detail about what each dollars job is for that month.

Then, each month, you could count out the money for each fixed expense and place it in an envelope at the right time of the month and send it in. You could gather the cash for your house payment and send it in when due. You could make your car payment in cash, pay your power bill in cash, and send cash to the insurance company. If you really wanted to, you could make everyone of your fixed reoccurring payments by pulling the cash out of the pot and making sure you get it there on time.

You could have your Airborne Unit (Household Expenses) in your box at all times. You could dole it out to your spouse as needed, carry it around in your wallet, or keep it in your shoe. I recommend you keep it in the bank and only get the cash out you need to spend for the week. Using cash is a great idea and will help control your spending. Carrying a lot of cash all the time can lead to trouble.

You would need to keep the Cavalry and Reserve boxes in a secure location and out of reach. Choosing to go manual defeats the goal of becoming lean, efficient, and effective with your finances.

Don't be afraid of banks. The technology is tight, the funds are secure, and the processing is smooth. Ease of implementation, ease of operation, and ease of communication. Those are the markings of a Battle Ready Budget.

Battle Ready Training Task 3.1

Build Your Own Battle Ready Budget

Sticking to a budget is a mission critical item. Using the resources located at www.battlereadyfinance.com, set up your initial budget.

Budgeting well is a learned skill and may take some trial and error before you have the system down cold. Don't give up. Work the numbers, use the calendar, and divide your bills, expenses, and income into the four accounts discussed.

If you have not done so already, now is the time to establish the accounts. Here is a list of what is needed:

1. Checking Account with Full Automation and limited Withdrawal Capabilities.

- This is your Fixed Bills Account.

- No checks or debit cards are needed.

- Set up automatic deposits with your employer or your bank in the amount needed only to cover your monthly fixed bills.

- Set up automatic withdrawals for every bill possible.

- This account should zero out at the end of every month.

2. Checking Account with Limited Automation and Full Withdrawal Capabilities

- This is your Household Expenses Account.

- Checks, debit cards, and cash withdrawals will be utilized.

- Set up automatic deposits with enough to cover your monthly expenses plus a cushion.

- There are no automatic withdrawals from this account.

- This is the account you will live out of. You control what comes out and when.

- This account may have carryover of cushion in any given month.

3. Savings Account with Limited Automation and Limited Withdrawal Capabilities.

- This is your Emergency Expense Account.

- Checks and transfers to the Household Expense account may be utilized.

- Set up automatic deposits to meet your monthly savings goals in order to fully fund this unit.

- There are no automatic withdrawals from this account.

- This account is for emergency expenses only. Utilize only when necessary.

4. Savings Account with Limited Automation and Limited Withdrawal Capabilities.

- This is your Savings Account.

- Checks and transfers to the Household Expense account may be utilized.

- Set up automatic deposits to meet your monthly savings goals in order to fully fund this unit.

- There are no automatic withdrawals from this account.

- This account is for known long and short term savings goals.

Many people reading this may only be able to set up the first two accounts with no resources available to fund an Emergency or Savings account. If that is the case, do what you can. Get started using this system and as you gain control of your finances, you will locate the resources needed to open the other accounts.

Chapter 4

Build Battle Ready Savings

"Go to the ant, you slacker! Observe its ways and become wise. Without leader, administrator, or ruler, it prepares its provisions in summer; it gathers its food during harvest."
Proverbs 6:6-8

While you may or may not currently be in a position to fully fund your Emergency and Savings accounts, it is critical that you understand the necessity of having those units available.

The concept of building and maintaining a Reserve Unit began with the US Army in 1908 with the idea that a civilian force would be able to complement the regular Army should a national emergency make it necessary. A Reserve Medical Corps was formed as the first civilian force under control of the Federal Government.

In 1912, the Army Appropriations Act approved the first full Regular Army Reserve as the US recognized the need to have a trained fighting force ready to support the regular Army. Congress understood having all of the nation's resources deployed opened the country to attack from other enemies and took action to ensure the US would not be left vulnerable.

While the US may have multiple enemies that could band together and bring the fight to the country from multiple directions, you have one enemy with a massive fighting force united against you. You have no need to wonder if you will be attacked; you can be assured the attacks are coming and indeed are under way.

The 1912 Congress needed to have hearings, debates, and lengthy discussion to settle the need for a Reserve Unit. You need to have no such debate. The building of your Reserve Unit (Savings) is not open for discussion, it is a proven need.

When I counsel with people about their finances, especially those who have debt, they often will justify their lack of savings in multiple ways. The most common is the idea that if there is a debt on the books with a high interest rate and money in a savings account with a low interest rate, it makes more sense mathematically to pull the savings and pay off the debt. Doing so saves interest, eliminates stress, and frees the resources that were being saved to make the payments on the debt.

Mathematically, that appears to be a very strong argument. **In fact, before I began to understand how money truly works and the nature of the battle, I made that argument as well**.

Carrying a debt at 10% interest while keeping money in the bank earning .25% interest seemed to go against common sense. Why pay the extra interest and add money to the Reserve Unit (Savings) when that money could be used to pay down the high interest debt?

While math is the justification used to support this argument, what does the math really show?

We probably know the answer, but it is good to get in the habit of checking your assumptions.

The Math of Debt

Consider a $10,000 credit card debt at 9.9% on which you are making a $125 minimum payment. It will take 11 years to take care of the debt and have it paid off and the total cost will be $16,413. That means you will pay $6,413 in interest over the life of the loan.

The total you are schedule to pay in interest alone on your debt is $6,413.07.

The total of all current loans and credit card payments are $125.00. If you continue to make the minimum payments it will take you 11 years to payoff this debt. The total interest paid will be $6,413.07.

Time to pay off debt is 11 years.   [·]

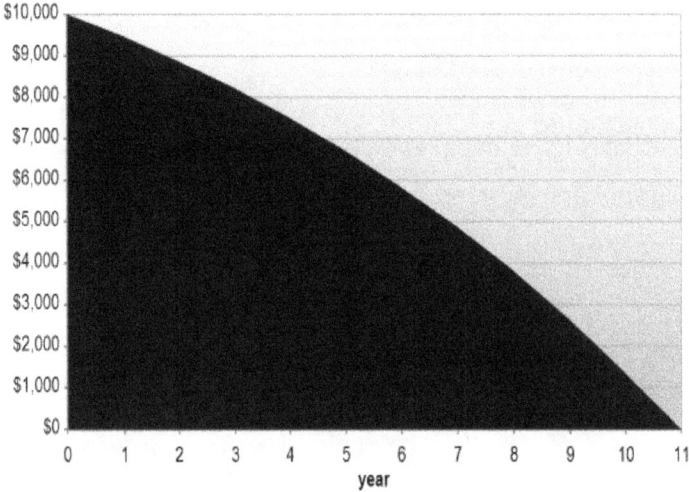

An Extra $100

Adding an extra $100 a month to the payment and sending $225 per month to the credit card company will reduce the time to retire the debt to 56 months, or just shy of 5 years.

The total spent to pay off the debt would be $12,508. The extra $100 a month will save you $3,905 in interest and shave 6 years off the time it takes to pay the debt.

When looking only at the cost of the debt and the time it takes to retire the debt, it is clear you should be sending an extra $100 a month to the credit card company.

Result Summary	
Total outstanding debt	$10,000.00
Monthly payment	$225.00
Average interest rate	9.9%
Total interest	$2,508.53
Time to pay off debt	4 years and 8 months

The Math of Savings

Before we make the decision to forgo savings and send the $100 to our credit card company, what other factors should be considered?

Because we live in a world where bad things happen and we have an enemy trying to make things even worse, we need to dig a little deeper.

Once you decide to take control of your finances, you can expect the fighting to intensify. Prepare to be hit at your weak points. When climbing out of debt by using 100% of your resources to do so, a glaring weakness is your ability to respond to new emergencies.

Some call it Murphy's Law, others just call it life, but whatever you call it, you can count on the fact that if you have no money saved, you will find a greater need for extra money.

When the car breaks down and you have no money, no Cavalry Unit (Emergency Fund) to come to the rescue, how do you pay the bill? When the air-conditioner in your home quits in mid-August how to you pay the repair man? When the unknown unknowns happen, how do you take care of them?

Much of the time, the answer is "by taking on more debt." Borrow money from the in-laws, use the credit card, or get a personal loan. Whatever the source, the need to solve the problem will outweigh the need to stick to your Victor-Six and further in debt you will go.

So, what is the alternative?

Looking back at the $10,000 debt scenario, let's consider what it looks like if we save the $100 a month and pay $125 toward the credit card. Stay with me here. I know this is a new way to think about debt and I am not necessarily telling you it is better hang on to debt. A Battle Ready Warrior will gather all relevant information before making a decision to act. You need to check the numbers.

Making a $125 monthly payment, we saw earlier that it will take 11 years and cost $16,413 to pay the debt.

How much could you save by putting $100 a month in a savings account over the same time frame?

Your savings could be worth $13,487.13 after 11 years.

If you save $100.00 per month your savings may grow to $13,487.13 after 11 years. This includes a starting balance of $100.00 and a 0.25% annual rate of return.

Balance by Year   [-]

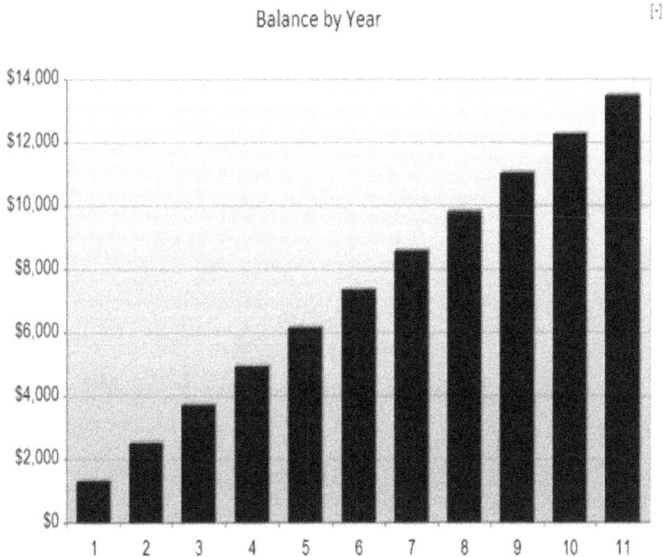

Saving $100 per month in an interest bearing account paying .25% per year would allow you to save $13,487.13 during the time it takes to pay off your credit card. To save or not to save, that is the question.

The Math of Waiting

If you decided it was better to save $100 a month for emergencies and you could get .25% interest, you could save $13,487 over an 11 year period. This number represents the cost of waiting or the "opportunity cost" of paying the extra money on the debt and forgoing the savings. What this means to you is that if you choose to only focus on the debt and decide not to save any money, you will have given up the opportunity to have accumulated $13,487 along the way.

If you were truly focused on the debt and you diligently applied the extra money to paying it down, you would reduce the opportunity cost by eliminating the debt early.

If you pay the debt fast and then in 4 years and 8 months begin saving the $100 a month? What does that look like? How much savings do you give up if you wait almost 5 years to start?

Results Summary		
	Start Now	Start Later
Starting amount	$100	$100
Savings plan	Save $100 per month for 6 years.	Postpone saving for 5 years then save $100 per month for 1 year.
Rate of return	0.25%	0.25%
Ending balances	$7,356	$1,303
Cost of waiting	$6,053	

Battlefield Decisions

With this information, we now have a decision to make. Do we choose to "lose" $6,129 in potential savings by knocking the debt out in 5 years and forego saving any money? Or is it better to spend $6,413.07 in interest payments by paying the debt slowly over the next 11 years?

In simple terms, here is the choice:

A.   Concentrate all your efforts on the debt and at the end of 5 years, you can have $0 debt and $0 savings.

B.   Make the minimum payment on the debt and put the extra toward savings. At the end of 11 years you can have $0 debt and $13,487 savings.

Which would you prefer?

The answer is really not as important as learning to think about debt and savings in this light.

Critical thinking about how you deploy your resources is a hallmark of a Battle Ready Financial Warrior. Making a decision without clearly understanding the repercussions is a common cause for difficulty.

For some, the level of stress caused by carrying debt is very damaging. Debt is viewed as evil and never to be used. The mere fact they have debt makes them physically ill. If you are one of those people, the answer for you may be to pay off your debt as quickly as possible hoping that nothing requiring extra money will crop up causing you to take on more debt.

Others really do not view debt as a problem and it does not cause them to worry or fret. They see it as a necessary evil and lose no sleep over a $10,000 credit card balance. If that is your view, saving the $100 may be a better choice. You will be prepared for the unexpected events that crop up.

Many people will fall somewhere in the middle. While you may not stress continually over debt, having it does make you uneasy but you also recognize the need to save. For you, paying the debt off AND saving money seems to make the most sense.

Result Summary	
Total outstanding debt	$10,000.00
Monthly payment	$175.00
Average interest rate	9.9%
Total interest	$3,580.25
Time to pay off debt	6 years and 6 months

The best answer may be to do both. Pay extra on your debt and put money in savings. By saving $50 a month and adding $50 a month to your minimum payment you will pay the debt off in 6 years and 6 months while accumulating $3,975 in savings. The interest paid would be $3,580, giving you $395 in net gain.

This allows you to save $600 a year while your debt is being reduced. Now you have given yourself a third choice when making the decision about your debt:

C.   Split your resources and attack both targets so that at the end of 6 years and 6 months, you can have $0 debt and $3,687.20 in savings.

Savings Balance

Year	Additions	Interest	Balance
Start	$50.00		$50.00
1	$600.00	$0.91	$650.91
2	$600.00	$2.46	$1,253.37
3	$600.00	$3.93	$1,857.30
4	$600.00	$5.46	$2,462.76
5	$600.00	$6.97	$3,069.73
6	$600.00	$8.47	$3,678.20
7	$600.00	$10.02	$4,288.22

Not a bad compromise and the important thing is when the attacks come, you have a Cavalry (Emergency Fund) and a Reserve Unit (Savings) that can be deployed.

Some of you may disagree here and that is okay. My goal is to train you to think and understand the outcomes of the possible decisions.

A better choice than all three scenarios is avoiding debt in the first place.

Debt is a destructive force that often brings years of suffering. It can alter your thinking, destroy your relationships, and change your personality. It is a dark cloud hanging over your life that will rain down pain at every opportunity. Debt clouds your judgment, distorts your Victor-Six-Vision, and makes it difficult to think beyond your current need to pay it off. The bible says the borrower is slave to the lender and if you carry a debt load, you no doubt recognize the truth contained in this scripture.

Assuming you have sufficient income to make minimum payments on your debts, fund your savings and emergency accounts, and have a little left over each month to attack you debts, what's the best method of getting rid of debt?

A commonly taught method made popular by Dave Ramsey is the Debt Snowball. Using this method, you order your debts from smallest to largest, regardless of the time commitment or interest rates. The idea is to make minimum payments on all your debts with the exception of the smallest one. To attack the smallest debt, you apply all extra money from your monthly budget to paying off the first and smallest debt. This is continued until the first debt is retired.

Once that has been accomplished, all of the money that was being used to pay off the first debt is added to the minimum payment for the second debt. Now you have the minimum payment + the payment amount for the retired debt + extra money from the budget for debt payoff. This larger amount is applied to the second debt until it is also retired.

Now that two debts have been eliminated, the same amount of monthly payment that was used to pay off those debts is added to the minimum payment of the third debt and this ever growing monthly payment amount (hence the name **Debt Snowball**) is applied until the third debt is paid in full.

This process continues until all debts are paid off.

Take a look at an example of the traditional Debt Snowball.

		Entry Columns			Calculated Columns	
#	Creditor	Balance Owed ($)	Interest Rate (%)	Payment Amount ($)	Interest Cost	# of Pmts Left
1	Discover	1000	9	85	$50.89	13
2	Paydayloan	3000	19	125	$804.01	31
3	Mom	4500	7	200	$338.14	25
4	Mastercard	6000	14	120	$3,057.42	76
5						
6						
7						
8						
9						
10						

Enter a monthly dollar amount you can add to your debt payoff plan: 200

Calculate Debt Snowball   **Clear Form**

Results	Balance Owed	Interest Rate	Payment Amount	Interest Cost	# of Pmts Left
Current totals:	$14,500.00	N/A	$530.00	$4,250.46	76
Debt Snowball Totals:	$14,500.00	N/A	$730.00	$1,867.34	23
Time and interest savings from Accelerated Debt Payoff Plan:				$2,383.13	53

The total of your current monthly debt payments ($530.00), plus the additional monthly amount of $200.00, is equal to $730.00. This is how much you will allocate to paying off your debts until all of the above debts are paid off.

Using the Debt Snowball in the example above, your debts could be eliminated 53 months faster by adding $200 extra per month to the snowball while saving $2,383.13 of interest.

The advantage of the Debt Snowball is that it can help you build momentum quickly by seeing early success. Paying off your smallest debt first can give you the motivation to continue using the snowball method until you have knocked out all of your debts.

Getting to the place where you can finally cut of those credit cards and experience total freedom from the chains of debt can give you an incredible sense of accomplishment and propel you forward to a great financial future.

An alternate method is to order your debts not from smallest to largest but from highest interest rate to lowest interest rate. We'll call it the **Interest Rate Snowball**. The same method used in the Debt Snowball is now applied to paying off the debts. Make the minimum payment on all debts except the one with the highest interest rate. For this debt, use all extra money from the monthly budget to pay the debt off as quickly as possible. Once the debt is retired, apply the monthly payment amount to the next debt with the highest interest. Continue until all debts are eliminated.

This method will result in paying your debts off in a similar time frame as the Debt Snowball but will save some money in interest as you move through the process.

Using the Interest Rate Snowball and adding the same $200 to the debt would result in paying off the debt 53 months faster while saving $2,501.61 of interest.

As compared to the Debt Snowball method, the Interest Rate Snowball will accomplish the goal in the same amount of time while saving $118 in interest.

Mathematically, the Interest Rate Snowball makes more sense, but as we have discussed, when dealing with your own financial battle sometimes more than just the numbers need to be taken into account. As the Battlefield Commander, it is up to you to examine all avenues of attack and then determine which will best help you accomplish your mission.

#	Creditor	Entry Columns			Calculated Columns	
		Balance Owed ($)	Interest Rate (%)	Payment Amount ($)	Interest Cost	# of Pmts Left
1	Paydayloan	3000	19	125	$804.01	31
2	Mastercard	6000	14	120	$3,057.42	76
3	Discover	1000	9	85	$50.89	13
4	Mom	4500	7	200	$338.14	25
5						
6						
7						
8						
9						
10						

Enter a monthly dollar amount you can add to your debt payoff plan: 200

Calculate Debt Snowball   **Clear Form**

Results	Balance Owed	Interest Rate	Payment Amount	Interest Cost	# of Pmts Left
Current totals:	$14,500.00	N/A	$530.00	$4,250.46	76
Debt Snowball Totals:	$14,500.00	N/A	$730.00	$1,748.85	23
Time and interest savings from Accelerated Debt Payoff Plan:				$2,501.61	53

The total of your current monthly debt payments ($530.00), plus the additional monthly amount of $200.00, is equal to $730.00. This is how much you will allocate to paying off your debts until all of the above debts are paid off.

While both the Debt Snowball and the Interest Rate Snowball work very well, you may need to consider a third approach.

Some debts, regardless of the size or interest rate, come with bad emotional baggage and should be attacked first. These are usually debts that have been the result of bad decisions, bad luck, bad behavior, or a mixture of all of the above. They serve as continual reminders of your mistakes and need to be paid off as quickly as possible.

These Bad Baggage Debts could be from a failed business, a momentary lack of judgment, a bad decision driven by emotion, or any number of life circumstances.

However you accumulated them, you need to get these out of your life. In the **Bad Baggage Snowball** you order your debts from the most painful or regretful to the least, regardless of amount or interest rate. Once the order is determined, use the same method as the other Snowballs to pay down the debts.

Emotions play a major role in the way your handle your money. The sooner you can eliminate destructive emotions regarding your money, the sooner you can move to a place of freedom.

As you move through this process, keep in mind that your mistakes do not define who you are, do not determine your future, and only control your present if you allow it. Remember the words of Paul who said *"But one thing I do, however, is to forget what is behind me and do my best to reach what is ahead. So I run straight toward the goal in order to win the prize, which is God's call through Christ Jesus to the life above."* Phil 3:13b-14

#	Creditor	Balance Owed ($)	Interest Rate (%)	Payment Amount ($)	Interest Cost	# of Pmts Left
		Entry Columns			Calculated Columns	
1	Mom	4500	7	200	$338.14	25
2	Paydayloan	3000	19	125	$804.01	31
3	Mastercard	6000	14	120	$3,057.42	76
4	Discover	1000	9	85	$50.89	13
5						
6						
7						
8						
9						
10						

Enter a monthly dollar amount you can add to your debt payoff plan: 200

Calculate Debt Snowball   **Clear Form**

Results	Balance Owed	Interest Rate	Payment Amount	Interest Cost	# of Pmts Left
Current totals:	$14,500.00	N/A	$530.00	$4,250.46	76
Debt Snowball Totals:	$14,500.00	N/A	$730.00	$2,022.36	23
Time and interest savings from Accelerated Debt Payoff Plan:				$2,228.10	53

The total of your current monthly debt payments ($530.00), plus the additional monthly amount of $200.00, is equal to $730.00. This is how much you will allocate to paying off your debts until all of the above debts are paid off.

Using the Bad Baggage Snowball with an extra $200 added will result in paying the debts off 53 months faster while saving $2,228.10 of interest.

As you can see, all three methods result in paying off the entire debt of $14,500 in 53 months. There is a few hundred dollars difference of interest either paid or saved, depending on the snowball used.

The big payoff comes when using the Bad Baggage Snowball in the form of emotional freedom. While financial freedom is the goal, the earlier you can rid yourself of the emotional baggage tied to yesterday's mistakes, the better off you will be.

The ability to forget what lies behind and focus on what lies ahead is both a spiritual discipline as well as an act of the will.

Your trust in God gives you the ability to believe for a better future. Your ability to take your thoughts captive allows you to focus on that future instead of the mistakes of the past.

Getting rid of the reminders (those bad debts) goes a long way in helping you move on mentally, emotionally, and spiritually.

Implementation

What if there is no extra money and minimum payments are all you can make?

Just as the US Congress in 1912 understood the danger of deploying 100% of the fighting force, so should you recognize the danger. Your enemy is very observant.

He has no ability to ready your mind, he is not all knowing, and he cannot be everywhere at once. He is limited in power, has no authority over you, and is defeated by the blood of Jesus Christ and he knows it.

Fighting from a position of defeat, he rallies his troops to locate weak points in your life and focus the attacks in the areas that will bring the most destruction. When you have no Cavalry Unit (Emergency Fund) or Reserve Unit (Savings), maximum pain can be inflicted by attacking your finances.

The question becomes, "where do we find the resources to build a Cavalry and Reserve?" The truth is there are no easy answers when you are in this position. If your resources are fully deployed, finding extra funds may be difficult. It may require you to get creative, take on extra work or extra shifts, sell some stuff, or start a side business.

While covering all the ways to find extra resources, stay calm in battle, and fight your way out of debt are beyond the scope of this chapter, you can find these topics covered in Appendix A: *Firefight* .

A few quick ideas that you can deploy immediately to build your Reserves:

Ideas for Quick Savings

Kill the Cable = $75 monthly savings

Brown Bag for Lunch = $100 monthly savings per person

Carpool with a co-worker = $100 monthly savings

Reduce Cell Phone Data Plan = $20 monthly savings

Keep Cell Phone Data and Eliminate Home Internet = $30 monthly savings

Eliminate Home Phone Service = $35 monthly savings

Shop with Coupons = $50 – $100 monthly savings

Raise Your Insurance Deductibles = $300 – $500 yearly savings

Dry Your Clothes on A Line Outside = $15 monthly savings

Drink Your Morning Coffee at Home = $40 monthly savings

Ideas for Quick Earnings

Have a Yard Sale = $200 – $300

Rake Leaves or Mow Yards = $25 - $50 per job

Lease a Room in Your Home = $150 per month

Offer Handyman Services = $20 per hour

Work a Part-Time Job = $250 - $300 per week

Sell Your DVD or CD collections = $20 -$100

Baby sit, House sit, or Pet sit = $15 - $50

Sell Used Electronics on Craigslist or EBay = $10 – $250

Use these lists to brainstorm ways you can quickly begin saving and building your Calvary (Emergency Fund) and Reserve (Savings) Units.

Assuming your income is sufficient to meet your obligations, the easiest way to begin building your Cavalry and Reserve Units is to plug the leaks. In most cases, when a good Battle Ready Budget is created, separating all of your fixed expenses from your variable expenses will allow you to easily see where money is slipping from your hands. Placing the fixed costs in your Infantry Unit will allow you to ensure those needs are met while you focus on the variable spending with the Airborne Unit.

Remember, the Airborne Unit holds all the resources you need for daily spending. Food, gas, utilities, clothes, and anything else that is not a fixed expense is taken care of by the Airborne Unit. When you find that your Airborne Unit continually has a need for more resources, see it as an opportunity to plug the leaks and become lean.

Suppose you have examined your variable spending over the last three months and have determined you spend $375 on groceries, $60 on fast food, $85 on dining out, $25 on entertainment, $75 on gas, and $55 on clothes each month. You add a $50 cushion for a total of $725 in the Airborne Unit. You are confident your unit is fully equipped to handle the task.

As the month rolls on, you find that somewhere around week 3, the Airborne Unit is hurting. Resources are quickly running out and there is still work to be done. You add an additional $100 to the account from the Reserve or Cavalry Units and finish out the month.

If this scenario takes place more than a few times, chances are you have an opportunity. You have two choices:

First, you could simply overfund your Airborne Unit to ensure there is never a shortage of resources. While this course of action may solve the immediate need, it does nothing to move you closer to operating at top efficiency. Remember, the Battle Ready Financial Warrior is one who is lean, efficient and effective. Building a bloated Airborne is counterproductive and self-indulgent. Not only does it run counter to your Victor-Six, it also sabotages your ability to build your Cavalry and Reserve Units.

The second course of action is far more difficult. The best thing to do when you find your Airborne is continually in need of resources before the monthly mission is complete is to look closely and find the inefficiencies. They are there and you will discover them if you choose to see them. We all have them. A quick cup of coffee and a biscuit in the morning, a few trips to the vending machine in the break room during the day, an unexpected lunch invitation with a friend, a pack of smokes, and a 20 oz. soda for the commute home. Suddenly $20 -$25 is missing from your pocket and the Airborne Unit feels the pain. Repeat this scenario once a week and the money runs out before the month is over.

You must track your variable spending and find the escape routes your funds are using to disappear. There are numerous smart phone apps that can be used to track spending. As an alternative, you can use a note pad to record all your daily spending over the next month to identify your spending patterns and habits.

Automate

Once you have used found the extra money by selling stuff, working more, and plugging the leaks, the key to successfully funding your Cavalry (Emergency Expenses) and Reserve (Savings) Units is Automation. As the battlefield commander, is it up to you to determine where to deploy new resources that come under your control. These decisions should be made once and then set up to happen automatically.

Making the decision to deploy 5% of new resources to the Cavalry Unit and 10% to the Reserve Unit is not a monthly decision. Once your Battle Ready Budget is complete, those decisions are made. The only action left is to direct either your employer or your bank to divide the money between the accounts you have chosen in the amounts you have selected.

Set it up to happen before you have the opportunity to spend the money and you can be assured when you need to call on the Cavalry or the Reserves, they will be there to support your mission.

Battle Ready Training Task 4.1

Locate Additional Resources and Determine Your Snowball Order

In this chapter, you have learned the importance of saving and have been shown how to make decisions about using debt. Your Battle Ready Training Task is to evaluate your current spending, locate additional funding, and begin to attack your debts.

Take a close look at all of your spending and determine if resources are being wasted. Use the calculators located at www.battlereadyfinance.com/debtcalculators to help determine the following:

- Evaluate your car payment to determine how quickly adding to the principal would eliminate the debt

- Use one of the debt snowball methods to reduce or eliminate credit card and other consumer debt. Use the Debt Snowball Calculator for assistance

- Determine how much can be saved by adding extra principal to your mortgage payment

Plug the leaks and redirect the resources to the appropriate unit for higher and better use. See if you can find and eliminate the following expenditures:

- Store or restaurant made coffee purchases

- Break room snack purchases

- Fast-food lunch purchases

- Impulse purchases

Take the following actions to locate more resources to meet your objectives:

- Evaluate your use of cable TV and its importance to your Victor-Six

- Examine your phone, internet, and cell phone bills for possible savings

- Discuss raising your insurance deductibles with your Insurance Company to realize possible monthly savings

- Consider a ride sharing or carpooling arrangement with a co-worker

Brainstorm on these and other ways to save money and implement as many as are workable for you and your family.

Chapter 5

Build Battle Ready Credit

"The rich rule over the poor, and the borrower is a slave to the lender." Proverbs 22:7

The word credit can be traced back to a Latin phrase meaning "I believe," an indication of the trust that is needed between the two parties in an agreement. The person lending resources has to believe the other person will repay the debt before the transaction can take place. When trust is established by either relationship or contract, the deal is made and a debt is created.

This is the very same idea which compels soldiers to take up arms and march into foreign lands to engage the enemy of their country. As a volunteer in the armed forces, trust is essential. A deep seated trust in the ideals of your country and a belief the leaders will uphold their end of the agreement. A soldier willingly trades his present in order to preserve his countrymen's future. His or her service ensures his friends and family will continue to enjoy freedom today though he knows he could be asked to pay the ultimate price to purchase this freedom. It is at great personal cost that our men and women in uniform carry this burden for us and our responsibility as a nation is to ensure we honor the debt by keeping the ideals they fight for alive.

The credit/debit relationship created between a soldier and a nation is one of the purest, most honest transactions which take place. The one who extends the credit, the soldier, does so knowing he may never collect. The one going into debt, the country, does so knowing it may never be able to repay the soldier or his family. The transaction takes place because both parties believe the sacrifice of future resources (the life of the soldier and his potential future contributions to society) is worth the current value received (the continued freedom of those he is fighting to protect).

While less than desirable, this type of credit is good and worthy. In order for a country to endure, there must always be those willing to pay freedom's price.

Just as the soldier gives up his future when he enters into the agreement with his country, the use of credit will demand you give up some of your future.

By its very nature, credit ties up your future resources in order for you to enjoy current benefits. You must be willing to agree to hand over a portion of your future earnings so that you can make current use of the product or service.

Credit then forces you to agree that the benefit you are receiving in the present is worth more than the unearned resources of the future.

Sometimes it is true and the current benefit outweighs the future cost. In this case, credit can be considered "good". Other times, the sacrifice of future resources for current use of a product is not worth the value the product is able to produce. This type of credit is "bad".

While good and bad are relative terms, with regard to credit there are some common rules that tend to apply. In general, using credit to purchase consumer goods is a bad idea. In most cases, the item being purchased begins to immediately decline in value meaning you would have a difficult time selling the item for enough to pay off the debt. Electronics, boats, motorcycles, household items, clothing, and automobiles all fall in this category.

On the other end of the equation are those things that could be considered "good" credit purchases. This list would include real property such as land, housing, and commercial buildings. In theory though not always in practice, these items increase in value and help to offset the cost of the loan. Using credit to make an investment into an appreciating asset should be the only acceptable use of borrowed money with very few exceptions.

Depending on where you are in life, you may wonder why all the discussion about the use of credit. Why devote an entire chapter just to tell you when to use or not use credit to make a purchase? If you have no experience with credit and the effects it can have on your life, it is difficult to understand the danger. Becoming aware of the traps before you enter the battle will better prepare you to avoid them.

The liberal use of credit to buy things you want but cannot yet afford is a common practice in our culture. The idea of waiting until the money has been saved and paying cash for items has been traded in for the ability to instantly gratify our wants and desires. Credit can create the appearance of wealth where no wealth exists while stealing part of your future income to pay for current needs. Do this often enough and you end up trading all of your future earnings to finance your current lifestyle. Credit breeds bad habits, limits your ability to save, and tricks you into believing you can have everything you want as long as you can afford the payments.

A standard sales practice for large ticket items is to talk about the monthly payments and not about the total cost of the item. When purchasing an automobile, the price may be $25,000 but the goal of the salesman will be to have you focus not on the price, but on the payment. He knows that it is much easier to make a $485 sale than to make a $25,000 sale. He will not engage you in conversation about the total cost of the car including interest payments, fees, the cost of insurance, maintenance and registration. He only wants you to decide that $485 fits into your monthly budget and you should drive the car home today.

However, you need to consider the total cost of ownership when purchasing anything on credit, especially large ticket items like cars, boats, electronics, etc. While the monthly payment may fit into your budget, agreeing to continue to pay over a 60 month period is not a good deal for you.

In order to determine how the purchase will impact your finances, you must strive to understand how much the car actually costs.

The Real Cost of Credit

Car Financing Summary	
Interest rate:	4%
Term in months:	60
Total purchase price (before tax):	$24,806.60
Taxable fees:	$0.00
Sales tax*:	$1,488.40
Non-taxable fees:	$40.00
Total sales price (after tax):	$26,335.00
Total down payment**:	$0.00
Amount financed:	$26,335.00
Monthly payment:	$485.00
Total payments***:	$29,099.96
Total interest paid***:	$2,764.96

A $24,806 car financed at 4% with nothing down will cost $29,099.96 over the life of the loan. Add $1500 per year for car insurance for 5 years and $300 -$500 a year in oil changes and maintenance, and the $25,000 car becomes a $40,000 car. The addition of these figures places to total monthly cost of ownership at $670. The question is not "can you afford the $485 monthly payment?," but should be "are you willing to take on the total $670 per month that the car will cost and does your budget have the extra resources?"

A much better way to drive a $25,000 car is to pay cash. If this is not an option for you, consider waiting until you have saved the money before buying the $25,000 new car. Making the choice to wait will help you learn to save, teach you to delay the gratification of your wants, and help you to build lifelong Battle Ready financial habits.

There is nothing wrong with driving a used car or truck. In fact, buying a new car off the lot is one of the worst financial decisions you can make. A car that is one year old has lost as much as 20% of its original value. After 5 years, the original value will have fallen by as much as 60%. Knowing this, a financial warrior will choose to buy a good used car and allow someone else to suffer the loss.

Why would you agree to borrow money and pay interest on an item that is depreciating at an average rate of 12% per year? A $25,000 loan at 3% interest for an item that loses 12% of its value on average per year causes you to lose 15% per year for the life of the loan.

If you were to decide to swallow your pride and drive a $5,000 car and save the money you would have spent had you purchased the $25,000 car, how long would it take to save enough to buy the $25,000 car for cash?

The total monthly cost of ownership for the new car was $640.00, which included the car payment of $485, car insurance of $125 per month, and oil changes and maintenance costs of $25 – $30 per month on average.

Buying the used car would allow you to save the payment of $485 and the insurance for the used car would be around $50 per month, saving an additional $75. You will still have maintenance costs for the used car, which could run more or less depending on the vehicle.

What that means to you is a total monthly amount of $560 hitting your Reserve Unit every month. After 48 months of delayed gratification, you will have accumulated $26,880, enough to buy a nice new car for cash if you choose to do so.

Alternatively, you could buy the same car you had wanted 4 years earlier, which would now have a sales price of $12,000, leaving $14,880 in your Reserve Unit.

Imagine the possibilities of living your life in this manner. If you buy the $12,000 car and continue to follow you savings habits for another 4 years, your Reserve Unit would grow to $41,760. Instead of falling victim to the worlds system of enslaving you with credit, you would live a life of freedom.

Freedom means having options when things go wrong. Freedom means going on vacation without incurring more debt. Freedom means looking at yourself in the mirror and knowing that you have made wise decisions. Freedom means self-respect and the confidence that comes knowing you have faced the best the enemy has to throw at you and you came out on top.

Obligating yourself to make monthly payments is a trap that can easily ensnare you if you are not paying attention. A car payment, a house payment, a credit card payment (or two or three), a store credit payment, and a personal loan may allow you to have everything you want right now. You can choose to live like everyone else and be just as miserable, or you can choose to live like a warrior who is courageous in the face of temptation, calm in the heat of battle, and prepared in the event of danger.

The best thing to remember about credit is that it is not necessary. One of the lies that have been propagated throughout our society is that each person should take steps to establish credit.

It sounds logical and always starts small. Open a low interest credit card with a low limit, just to show you can manage money. Buy your next TV on credit and then pay it off, just to establish a history of paying on time. Get your name in the system and develop a proven history of living up to your obligations. Do all of this so when you are ready to buy a house the lender will see you as a good credit risk.

While it is true that lenders will find it odd that you have no credit history, it does not mean you cannot buy a home. In general, lenders will look at your income, your assets, and your credit to determine if you are a good risk. Since you have no credit to speak of, you will need to have a steady income and some savings in your Reserve Unit. Unless you are just out of college or have been living rent free with your parents, you will have a rental history, a utility bill history, a phone payment history, and other payments that can establish your level of financial responsibility. Credit is not necessary to show that you are a good risk.

Noted scientist Albert Einstein once said "Compound interest is the eighth wonder of the world. He who understands it, earns it … he who doesn't … pays it." Specifically, he was talking about the long term effect of the time value of money. While this will be covered in more detail in *Battle Ready Finance: Advanced Training* on the chapter dealing with investing, it will serve you well to gain an understanding of how compounding interest works against you when you borrow money.

The Effects of Compounding Interest

In simple terms, compound interest means that when a dollar of interest is earned, that new dollar begins earning interest as well. An amount of $10,000 with daily compounding interest of 5% means that on the first day, the $10,000 will earn $1.37 of interest (5%/365 = .0001369 daily interest rate). On day two, the full amount of $10,001.37 will earn interest at the same 5 rate. The original $10,000 will earn another $1.37 and the first payment of $1.37 of interest will have earned interest at the same 5%/365 day rate. Each new interest paid also begins to earn interest. While the amount of interest paid on the interest that was earned each previous day starts out small, over time compounding can make a difference.

A credit card debt of $10,000 with simple interest of 18% will earn $1,800 of interest that will be paid at the end of the 1 year term. The same debt, compounded daily, will earn $1,971.64 of interest that is earned by the credit card company from you. The difference of $171.64 is the interest that the daily interest earns as it is added to the account balance. If you carried this debit for 10 years, the total owed would grow to $60,469.64 if compounded daily but only $52,338.36 if compounded annually.

This concept of compound interest, while maybe not yet clear enough for you to explain it in detail, should at least help open your eyes to the ravages of debt. High interest debt will snowball if left unpaid and could begin to accumulate faster than your ability to pay it off. You may find yourself caught in the minimum payment trap where each month, all you can do is pay on the interest that has earned interest with very little going toward the original debt itself. In fact, a debt of $10,000 compounding daily where only the minimum payment is made, will take you more than 30 years to pay off the original $10,000 debt because you have to pay over $25,000 in compound interest along the way.

Debt Summary						
	Balance	Interest Rate	Monthly Payment	Interest Paid	Total Payments	Time to Payoff
Credit card #1	$10,000.00	18%	$200.00	$25,112.50	$35,112.50	30 + years
Totals	$10,000.00	18%	$200.00	$25,112.50	$35,112.50	more than 30 years

Credit Is Not Your Friend

Maybe you are not a numbers person. As you read over the last several pages, the numbers may have kind of blurred together and you really just scanned the pages. If that's you, I need to be sure you get the message loud and clear.

> **Credit is not your friend. Credit will trick you, use you, take your money, and ruin your future. Avoid credit whenever you can.**

In combat, a leader's ability to make good decisions under intense pressure can be the difference between victory and defeat. Regardless of the amount of training, preparation, and capability of the troops, if the battlefield commander fails to correctly assess the situation and is out maneuvered by the opposing force, heavy causalities will be taken.

It is only when the leader keeps his head together, remains calm, and allows his training and that of his soldiers to kick in that he is successful. Emotions must stay under control and fear set aside. The battlefield commander learns to rest in the knowledge that he has the finest, best equipped, most dedicated, and most highly trained fighting force on the planet. He understands that if he does his job, uses sound judgment, and allows his men to do theirs, no enemy can defeat them.

As the battlefield commander in your own war, your decision making abilities will be tested time and again. You will face challenges, temptations, and struggles. They come at you from every direction, demanding courage and resolve. The world beckons with trinkets and distractions, pleading for you to give up the struggle and join the others as they blissfully stroll down a path of financial ruin. The trap is set, the bait is appealing, and entrance is unencumbered. The enemy is in position, waiting to strike at your first mistake, and credit is his weapon of choice.

This is your moment of victory or defeat. This is where your decisions determine the fate of your family. This is where your inner financial warrior must emerge. There will be no cheering crowd to urge you to make the right choice. There will be no hero's welcome for standing tall in the face of danger; there will only be you. Will you wake up tomorrow knowing that when faced with a challenge, though the pressure was immense, you held your ground and became stronger for the next fight?

Get this one thing right: learn to deal with and use credit in the right way. The intensity of the fight will lessen as you advance toward your target. Fall into the trap of credit, loading yourself with a string of monthly payments, and the enemy will punish you for years to come.

Most of us, me included, live under the delusion that if we only made more money, things would be so much better. We would be able to do more for our family, our church, and our community. We could alleviate the pressure that a lack of money exerts, and life would just be easier. What we fail to realize is that learning to manage what we have now and live within our means is the key to long term success. The ability to engage in the work that you have been called to do does not rely on the amount of income you earn, but rather on the amount of income you keep. You must create a margin between what you earn and what you spend. An income of $200,000 with expenses of $210,000 will not allow you to fulfill your mission. Though you earn a big income, there is no margin. There is nothing left except stress and struggle.

"It's better to have one handful of tranquility than to have two handfuls of trouble and to chase after the wind". Ecc. 4:6

Don't chase after the wind. Don't chase after something that cannot be caught. Using credit to create an allure of wealth is an illusion. Buying things to make you feel better, to impress your neighbors, or to satisfy your cravings will leave you empty, angry, and dejected.

Find your self-worth in what God has put inside of you and pursue it. Develop those gifts, using them to serve others, and you will find the peace and joy that no amount of stuff can bring.

Getting more is not the answer, but giving more is. Learn to live within your means, learn to give with a cheerful heart, learn to love others as you love yourself, and peace will be your constant companion.

Yes, you will still experience heartache and things won't always go your way. You will still make mistakes and will suffer the consequences. However, if you will determine to avoid debt whenever possible, you will place yourself and your family in the best possible position to withstand the blows of the enemy.

I promised in the beginning to tell you the one critical skill that would serve you above all others in your pursuit to become a Battle Ready Financial Warrior.

Well, this is not that thing, but it ranks a very close second.

There are few things in your life that will ruin your financial future faster than the use of credit and out of control spending.

Be very cautious, very wise, and very hesitant when considering the use of credit.

Keep reading for the one thing that can render you financial future impenetrable by the enemy and his devices.

Battle Ready Training Task 5.1

Evaluate Your Use of and Attitudes About Credit

If you are not yet convinced that credit is a dangerous weapon, at least take a close look at its place in your life. Your Battle Ready Training Task is to take a hard look at your credit profile.

1. Compile a list of all open credit accounts and the total amount available and then ask yourself the following questions:

- If the full amount of the available credit were in use, would I be concerned?

- Could I make the required monthly payment if I maxed out any one of the credit accounts? (usually 4% of the balance is the required minimum monthly payment)

- Why do I have this much credit available if I do not intend to use it?

- If I do intend to use it, am I ready for the consequences?

- Am I maintaining this credit for a sense of security?

2. Evaluate the answers to the above questions and take the appropriate actions:

- Close accounts as necessary to move to an acceptable level of credit that is available for use

- If you keep credit accounts open, make all decisions regarding their use and then stick to the rules

Should you find that credit has already consumed you and you are in the middle of battling to make the monthly payments, read Appendix A: *Firefight* for ideas on how to stay calm in the fight and move forward with a purpose.

Chapter 6

Deploy Your
Secret Weapon

"Honor the Lord with your possessions and with the first produce of your entire harvest; then your barns will be completely filled, and your vats will overflow with new wine." Proverbs 3:9-10

There are few things that a battlefield commander desires in combat more than a distinct tactical advantage. If he can know something the enemy does not know, possess weapons the enemy does not possess, or have the edge in training and the preparedness of his men, the odds are stacked in his favor.

A commander with superior firepower and confidence in his troops is a force to be reckoned with. Add experience and accurate information about the tactics of the enemy and there will be nothing that can stand in the way of completing the mission.

Untold billions if not trillions of dollars are spent by governments every year in an effort to develop the latest and greatest military weapons. Building the most highly trained force and equipping them with the most technologically advance weapon systems has been the goal as long as human governments have been on the earth. With the premise of protection for their people and peace for their land, military might is established as a way to keep invaders at bay and to respond by force if necessary. Peace through superior firepower.

In the life of the follower of Christ, there are multiple weapons that have been given to fight our battle. We are told in scripture to *"Put on the full armor of God, so that you can take your stand against the devil's schemes"* Eph 6:10.

We are given a full set of armor to protect us, if only we will choose to wear it. *"Stand firm then, with the belt of truth buckled around your waist, with the breastplate of righteousness in place, and with your feet fitted with the readiness that comes from the gospel of peace. In addition to all this, take up the shield of faith, with which you can extinguish all the flaming arrows of the evil one.*

Take the helmet of salvation and the sword of the Spirit, which is the word of God." Eph 6:14-17

We are well equipped, just as any solider should be, to face the enemy head on. We have all the tools necessary to engage in warfare. We have protection from attacks as well as weapons to launch our own attack. We face a defeated enemy; we yield the authority of The Lord of Lord and King of Kings. Greater is He that is in us than he that is in the world.

That has got to be the greatest tactical advantage in the history of warfare. We possess authority and power that the enemy forces do not possess.

What else do we have that they do not have? What do we know that they do not know? How can we be better prepared than those forces that are coming against us?

While the answers to those questions are numerous and our advantage is great, for the purpose of this discussion, we will focus on one distinct action we can take that will greatly multiply our power in battle and our effectiveness in life. The bible tells us that we have a "secret weapon" we can deploy to ensure we walk in victory in our financial lives. This weapon, when yielded correctly, will cause the attacks of the enemy to become ineffective, strengthen your resolve in battle, increase your faith in trials, and keep you mentally prepared to face each new challenge.

This is the One Thing, the one critical skill that has the power to transform your entire financial future.

The Power of Giving

Sacrifice. A word we throw around a lot when we talk about our men and women in uniform. We recognize that they must give up many of the things we take for granted when joining the service. They give up the freedom to go and do as they please and instead submit themselves to the orders of their commander. They give up time with family and friends, often for months and years on end. They forsake careers, homes, and the possibility of wealth so that we may freely pursue all those things. They give. They give their time and talents to fight in places they have never heard of to protect people they do not know.

When a soldier is killed in combat, we say he has made the ultimate sacrifice. He gave his life in service to his country. He paid the high price of freedom on some foreign battlefield in some distant land. "All gave some, some gave all."

The willingness of the solider to freely give of himself is what brought us to the place we call freedom today. But it is not just the soldier who gave. Men and women throughout history have given up comforts and convenience to further the cause of freedom, to fight for the rights of others, or to shed light on the plight of the downtrodden.

It is by our very nature that we understand that at times we are called to give more than we think we can, to do more than our share, to carry more than our own load. Out of love for others, we sacrifice to make things better and bring about the change necessary to preserve our freedoms. We were created with a great capacity to give.

The greatest giver of all time is Jesus of Nazareth. Forsaking a Kingdom, He came in the form of a child. He lived the life of a carpenter's son in a normal family in a poor land. He suffered the hardships of life, faced the temptations all face, and dealt with the same troubles all deal with. He experienced everything we all experience. Hunger, thirst, lack, shame, rejection, hatred, sadness, physical pain, emotional distress; He dealt with it all. Yet through everything, He never reacted out of concern for self, but from love for others. He never failed, never lashed out without thinking, and never said anything He regretted. He lived a perfect life.

For 33 years, He was separated from His Father while He walked in a foreign land among the forces of the enemy. He gave up His relationships, His position, and His wealth. He gave it all up so that He could bring about the change necessary for all men to have freedom.

Freedom from the chains of sin, freedom from a meaningless life, and freedom from death.

Finally, He gave everything by going to the cross of Calgary and freely laying down His life so that you and I could enjoy the benefits of freedom and live in a right relationship with God the Father. He gave every last drop of His blood to pay the price. He paid a debt He did not owe so that we could receive a gift that we could not buy.

Jesus is the greatest giver of all time.

You have a legacy of giving which you inherited first from God, passed down through His son Jesus, and placed into all humanity. Sacrifices were made for you in order to give you all you have and all you will ever accomplish. Nothing that is good and right in your life is there except for the fact that someone made a sacrifice.

In your financial battle, you too are called to sacrifice. You are called to freely give so that others may receive the same freedom that has been offered to you; freedom from sin, freedom from a life without meaning, and freedom from death.

You are asked to give of your time, your talents, and your treasure so that the message of the Good News of Jesus Christ is spread throughout the world.

Giving money to a church or religious organization is becoming less common as we progress through the modern age. People in general and Christians specifically seem to be less willing to make the sacrifice of their money. They have become jaded by the misuse or the perceived misuse of resources and have decided to withhold what God has asked them to give. In doing so, many have missed the best of what God has in store for them.

Since the beginning of our history, God has compelled us to be givers. He asked Cain and Able, the first brothers born on earth, to give the best of their wealth, each in his own way and according to his own heart. Later, Abraham gave a tenth of all his plunder to a priest when he returned from battle as a way to honor God and thank Him for the victory. His grandson Jacob also made vows to God that he would give back a tenth of all he owned if God would only bless him.

They gave as a way of thanking God for all that He had done or would do for them. Before the law was written, before tithing was introduced, these men gave back a portion of what they owned to their God who they loved, and the legacy of giving was born.

What's In It for Me?

Unlike the solider who gives up everything with no promise of ever receiving anything in return or Jesus who sacrificed Himself to give others life, our giving comes with a promise. God tells us that if we will only trust Him, He will make it so that we receive back much more than we give. The opposite is also true. He tells us that if we withhold our giving and do not trust in Him to provide all that we need, things will not go well for us.

"You are under a curse—your whole nation—because you are robbing me. Bring the whole tithe into the storehouse, that there may be food in my house. Test me in this," says the Lord Almighty, "and see if I will not throw open the floodgates of heaven and pour out so much blessing that there will not be room enough to store it. I will prevent pests from devouring your crops, and the vines in your fields will not drop their fruit before it is ripe," says the Lord Almighty. 'Then all the nations will call you blessed, for yours will be a delightful land,' says the Lord Almighty." Malachi 3:9-12

Your capacity for giving combined with God's promised blessing on your life is you're "Secret Weapon". **When you give, not out of compulsion or out of a desire to manipulate God, but out of trust in His plan for your life and in His promises, He promises to cause amazing things to happen.**

Take a look at each section of the above scripture:

1.   *You are under a curse – your whole nation – because you are robbing me.* God, speaking through the prophet Malachi, was talking directly to His chosen people, the Israelites. They were

disobedient by refusing to give to help support the priests and as a result, God said they were stealing from Him and called them cursed. While they wanted to be blessed, by their actions they were cursed.

2.   *Bring the whole tithe into the storehouse, that there may be food in my house.* The word tithe simply means "a tenth". God had told them they were to give a tenth of all of their increase to the Levite priests in order to maintain the tabernacle (their place of meeting) and to take care of the needs of the priests. Not 2%, not 5%, not 9%, but 10%. They were told what to do, given clear instructions and reasons why, yet they refused to give what God required.

3.   *Test Me in this.* This is the only place in the entire Bible where you will find God inviting His people to test Him in anything. This issue of trusting Him and giving to support the work He wants done on earth is so important that asks His people to give Him a chance to show what He can do. In effect, He is saying "You don't believe I will do what I say? That's fine, but at least try it out and see if I don't come through. Test this theory and see if I don't make it so the 90% you keep goes further and does more than keeping it all for your selfish desires. I will do it, just watch".

4.   *And see if I will not throw open the floodgates of heaven and pour out so much blessing there will not be room to store it.* This is where it starts to get real. God, who owns everything, just dropped a bomb on His people. He says "here's what's going to happen guys.

First, I am going to go out and remove the barrier that has been holding back all of your blessings. I am not just going to open the gates, I will throw them open so that you don't get a stream, but you get it all rushing toward you at once. Next, as the flood comes, I am going to also empty all the containers in heaven that hold your blessing and add to what you are receiving. You are going to get so much, that you won't have room for it all. You will have to share it with others. You will have so much that you will have no choice but to give some away."

5.   *I will prevent pests from devouring your crops, and the vines in your fields will not drop their fruit before it is ripe.* When we think of blessings and giving, we almost automatically think money. For the Israelites, who lived in a time when food was hard to come by, their blessings were in crops and produce. They were an agricultural society and abundant crops would mean survival, sustainability, and security.

Money would be of little use if there were nothing to eat and no place to buy food. An abundant source of food would equal true wealth. God was saying "not only am I going to cause your crops to produce more than you can use and store and cause your vineyards to hang heavy with more grapes than you can imagine, I am also going to protect them. If you will just trust Me, I will bring in heavenly pest control to make sure nothing happens to the things I provide for you. I will make sure that you get it all. No enemy can take it, no accident can shake it, and no drought will bake it. I am giving it to you and I will take responsibility to make sure that you get every bit of it."

6.   *Then all the nations will call you blessed for yours will be a delightful land.* Here, God is promising to reverse the curse. Because they had failed to obey, they were living in a cursed land and everyone around them knew it. It was evident that things were not going well for God's chosen people. Their actions were reflecting poorly on God and He wants that to change. He wants all the people who look at His chosen ones to see that because they trust Him, love Him, and obey Him, their lives are blessed.

He says "look guys, right now your lives are bad and your neighbors can see that. They see that you are hungry and poor. They know that you are my people so work with Me here. Just do what I am telling you so that I can take care of you. They need to see what can happen when they learn to love Me and trust Me and you a mucking it all up. I can't bless your disobedience so get on board with my plan. Allow me to bless you so that others will be drawn to Me. Seriously, let me make things good for you so everybody can see it."

Can you begin to see how giving is such a strong weapon to use against your enemy? Not only will it cause God to allow more blessing to flow into your life, it will help bring others into His kingdom by seeing what He has done for you. People are watching you, just like they were watching the Israelites. They know you follow God and they want to see if it makes a difference. If your life is just as messed up as everyone else and you are struggling along with the rest of the crowd, how is that any better? How will that attract anyone to Him?

The people in your life need to see that because you have placed your trust and faith in God, things are different for you. Things just seem to work out for you. You always seem to have enough. You have something different about you and they want to be a part of

it. That is God's plan for you. He wants to bless you so that you can be a blessing for others.

Lest you think that tithing and blessing are Old Testament ideas and that God does not expect that or work like that anymore, read 2 Corinthians 9 in the New Testament. God says to His church through the apostle Paul *"The point is this: whoever sows sparingly will also reap sparingly, and whoever sows bountifully will also reap bountifully. Each one must give as he has decided in his heart, not reluctantly or under compulsion, for God loves a cheerful giver."*

Give because you want to be part of what God is doing. Give because you want to reap a bountiful harvest. Give because God asks you to trust Him. Give so that others can learn of God's love.

"He who supplies seed to the sower and bread for food will supply and multiply your seed for sowing and increase the harvest of your righteousness. You will be enriched in every way to be generous in every way, which through us will produce thanksgiving to God." 2 Corinthians 9:10

You will be enriched in every way to be generous in every way which will produce thanksgiving to God. You will be given enough that you can be generous to other people who will, because of what God has done in your life and your willingness to pour it into their life, will give thanks to God and turn to Him.

So, in the Old Testament, God tells us to bring in the full 10% so that the priests can be taken care of and so that He can pour out blessings on us. In the New Testament, He tells us through Paul to give whatever amount we have decided in our hearts and to do it cheerfully.

So it is 10% or whatever amount we feel good about giving? How much do we need to give?

In the Old Testament, God's people were first commanded by law to give 10% and then encouraged by God through the promise of blessings to just do what He asked them to do. He wanted them to be faithful, follow the law, and allow other nations to know that there is a God in Israel.

In the New Testament, Paul tells us to find out what God wants us to give, and give it willingly. How are we to know what He wants us to give?

One way to know is to look at the words of Jesus. In Luke 6:38 Jesus says *"give, and it will be given to you. Good measure, pressed down, shaken together, running over, will be put into your lap. For with the measure you use it will be measured back to you."*

A couple of things are going on here. First, Jesus is reiterating the promise that if we are obedient and give, God will pour out blessings in our lives.

If you think of buying a basket of wheat and trying to get as much as possible for your money, you would see the picture Jesus is painting. To get as much as the basket will possibly hold, you have to press it so the air pockets are gone, shake it down so it all settles into the nooks and crannies of the basket, and then mound it up on the top to call it full. If you move it too fast, the wheat will fall out into your lap.

If you are paying and you get to do the measuring, that's the way you would fill your own basket. That is the kind of blessing Jesus is describing, one like you would give yourself, only even more.

The second thing going on in that passage is that Jesus is telling us that if we are stingy with our giving, we will get a stingy blessing in return.

Go back to the basket of wheat. This time, you are the seller and not the buyer. A stingy seller will not press down the wheat, not shake the basket to get in as much as possible, and certainly will not mound it up. He will want to give as little as he can to and still get the full price of for the basket from the buyer. His measure of what is a full basket of wheat and the buyer who would fill their own basket would be quite different. The seller would be stingy to the buyer but the buyer would be generous to himself.

The last thing Jesus said in this passage is that the measure you use will be what is used to determine how much of a blessing you receive in return. If you are a stingy giver, you will get a stingy blessing. Give only the minimum that God asks you to give to still be in compliance with the law and you will receive only the minimum in return. Give extravagantly out of love for other people and trust in God and you will be blessed extravagantly.

Yes, It Is All About You

I don't want to give you the impression that you can manipulate God into giving you great blessings. This is not a "give in order to receive" teaching. The use of this Secret Weapon is about so much more than giving and receiving back from God.

When you give, it changes who you are on the inside; it transforms you. Giving takes your focus off of you and places it on others. It helps you learn to trust not in material things but in the love and provision of your Father.

Having lived a portion of my life as a non-giving believer, I am well aware of the things you might tell yourself to justify why you do not follow this particular teaching.

Trying to provide for a family is tough enough without giving a portion of your money away – money that could be used to buy food, pay debts, pay rent, saved for retirement, or a thousand other things. From a purely financial viewpoint, giving 10% or more of your income away doesn't seem to do much for your bottom line, especially if you are having a tough time making ends meet. Why would God want you to struggle and have even less money when He clearly doesn't need it? After all, He is the maker of heaven and earth and all that is in them. If He wanted money, all He needs to do is say the word. What then, could He possibly want with yours?

As it turns out, it is not really about the money at all. Money is just the thing that we modern humans place the most value on. It is the thing that we most want; the thing that we think will meet all of our needs, give us security, and cause our lives to work out right.

What God knows and what He wants us to realize is that no created thing can meet our needs, be our security, or cause or lives to work out like we want.

While money may temporarily feel like it is doing all of those things, sooner or later we all learn the truth. Some learn it by chasing money their entire lives only to realize, usually near the end, that money was not what they needed. Some learn it by acquiring a substantial amount of money only to find they are living empty lives devoid of meaning.

The truth is, money is a liar. Actually, it is not that money lies, but that the world system, controlled by the father of lies, works very hard to keep you convinced that all you need is more money.

Your enemy knows the truth as well. He knows that money cannot meet your needs, be your security, or cause your life to work out like you want. He knows that if he can get your focus on either how much or how little money you have and get you to spend all of your time worrying about money, he can keep you from learning the truth that only God can give you all those things. Money, though neutral on it's on, can be one of the most deadly weapons used against you.

However, when you learn the truth about money, it can also be your strongest weapon.

Let go of your dependency on money and become dependent on God and you will soon find money taking its proper place in your life. Instead of a thing to be craved, money will become a tool that you use to change the lives of other people.

The truth is, when you were created, you were given a void that only God can fill. You were made to crave a relationship with Him, to desire His presence, and to always seek His face as a way to fill that void.

However, as fallen humans in a fallen world, we have all been tricked into thinking that other things can fill the void. Money is just one of the countless substitutes we use to try and fill the emptiness. Materialism is our modern term for what scripture calls "the love of money."

You have no doubt heard it said that money is the root of all evil. This bit of scripture is often repeated as sage advice given to those who are struggling with some issue involving either too little or too much money. The problem with this "advice" is that it is completely wrong and is not what the Bible says.

Money is not evil nor is it the root of evil. Money, when it takes the right place in our lives, can be one of Gods most frequent blessings. His people, whom He loves and whom He placed in this world knowing full well the role money would play, need money. We need it in all areas of our lives. We need it to further His message around the world. Money is not the problem.

The scripture actually says that the LOVE OF MONEY is a root of all kinds of evil. Not the money, but the love of money. Placing your faith, trust, and hope in money is the root of all kinds of evil. Relying on money to make you happy, meet your needs, give you peace, and cause things to work out for you is a root of all kinds of evil.

Materialism is a disease and giving is the cure.

When you, by faith, begin to give away some of your money, you begin to change. Your view of money begins to change. When you can let go of the thing you have loved your entire life, you start to see money in a different light. You see it for what it is. A tool. A tool that when put in its proper place can radically transform your life and the lives of those around you.

When you let go of money as your security and grab hold of God, everything is different. The pressure to produce leaves your shoulders and falls on Gods, and His shoulders are much bigger. He can produce what you never could. He can come through when it looks like there is no hope. He can be the source of all you need, if you will only let Him.

Become a giver and watch as the smoke clears and the morning dawns. The battle will look different. The weapons you wield will have the power to transform a fierce battle into a minor skirmish. You will walk in victory only when you learn to walk with God and trust Him to meet your needs. Take up the weapon of Giving and take back what the enemy has stolen.

Same Actions Same Results

Albert Einstein, one of the greatest thinkers in history once gave this definition of insanity: "doing the same thing over and over again and expecting different results."

While insanity may be too strong of a word to use with regard to your decisions on how you handle your money, it is true that if you do not change your actions, you will not see change in your finances.

James, the brother of Jesus said "faith without works [action] is dead." The Message translation expands this statement in this way:

"Dear friends, do you think you'll get anywhere in this if you learn all the right words but never do anything? Does merely talking about faith indicate that a person really has it? For instance, you come upon an old friend dressed in rags and half-starved and say, "Good morning, friend! Be clothed in Christ! Be filled with the Holy Spirit!" and walk off without providing so much as a coat or a cup of soup—where does that get you? Isn't it obvious that God-talk without God-acts is outrageous nonsense?

I can already hear one of you agreeing by saying, "Sounds good. You take care of the faith department, I'll handle the works department."

Not so fast. You can no more show me your works apart from your faith than I can show you my faith apart from my works. Faith and works, works and faith, fit together hand in glove." James 2:14-18

Though you may desperately want things to be different and have the faith to believe they will be different, until you put into action the things you have learned, you will continue down the path you are on.

You were meant for more than that. You have a purpose for being here and it does not include constant financial struggle. There will be seasons in your life where difficulties come, where your faith is stretched, and where your metal is tested. Jesus said *"In this world you will have trouble, but take heart, I have overcome the world"*. We can be sure that life on this planet will not always be rainbows and roses.

However, Jesus also said *"The thief comes only to steal and kill and destroy. I came that they may have life and have it abundantly."*

When taken as a whole, scripture makes it very clear that you will have both times of hardship and times when things just seem to fall into place. You will have seasons of success and seasons of failure. You will experience joy and you will experience sadness. Such is life.

It is also clear that God wants to bless you, to give you good things, and to make your life go well for you. He wants happiness and peace for you. He loves you as His child and wants to give you good gifts. We are told that He has a plan for us, His children. A plan to give us a hope and a future. A plan to prosper us and not harm us. God is on our side and because He is for us, no one can really be against us.

Scripture is clear that God wants to bless you, but more than that, He wants to grow you into the person you are designed to be. He wants to mold you and shape you into the vessel He has envisioned.

This may mean that before you can be blessed and used for His purposes on earth, you have to be molded into a usable form. As you are shaped by the Masters hands and begin to conform to His design, you may have to go through the fires of adversity to be hardened so you will not crack with use. Blessings and happiness will come when you make the choice to become who God wants you to be.

For most of us, the only thing standing between where we are now and the life God has planned, is us. While we have an enemy we face daily, the reality is that he has been defeated. If we would only get out of our own way and get on board with God's plan, laying our plans to the side, our lives could be radically different.

Imagine you are a soldier getting ready to go to war. You have just completed training, have been issued your first round of live ammunition, and have been given orders that will put you right in the middle of the conflict. Facing injury and possible death, you stare into the distance wondering just what is waiting for you out there on the battlefield.

Will you stand and face the fight with courage or will you be overcome with fear? Will you remember your training and act in confidence or will you freeze up and forget all you have been taught? Will you ever see your family again?

As those thoughts bore through your mind and as you resign yourself to an unknown fate, you are startled by the voice of your commanding officer. "Listen up men!" he barks. "We have just learned some important information about the enemy we will be up against. As it turns out, they have no weapons that can hurt you. Nothing in their arsenal can do permanent damage. They have some things that can make you uncomfortable for a while. In fact, you may even have some temporary pain, but it won't last. Nothing they can do to you will have a lasting effect. There is nothing to be afraid of so let's get the job done and get on home to our families."

Imagine the change that would take place inside of you. Knowing that nothing the enemy could do to you would last, that nothing they could do would work, your whole attitude would change. You would go from a worried solider facing an unknown enemy to confident invincible fighting machine in a matter of moments. You would be itching to get into the fight, to take the enemy head on, and to collect the spoils of victory. It would be a glorious day to be a soldier.

In your life, in your fight, against your enemy, you are that soldier. In Isaiah 54:17 God says *"No weapon formed against you shall prosper, and every tongue which rises against you in judgment You shall condemn. This is the heritage of the servants of the Lord, and their righteousness is from Me,"* Says the Lord.

No weapon the enemy has to wield against you will have lasting success. Sure, you may take it on the chin from time to time. You may have to walk through the valley or sail through the storm, but it is only temporary. Your job is to keep fighting, keep walking, and keep moving forward.

With God's righteousness, that is a right standing with Him through a relationship with Jesus, you are invincible. The mere sight of you makes the devil shake in is flaming red boots. You are a force to be reckoned with, a solider in the army of the Most High, and you will not be defeated.

Cast financial worries aside, apply the principles you have learned, and tell your adversary to take a hike. You've got this. God has already decreed it to be so.

Battle Ready Training Task 6.1

Learn to wield this Secret Weapon well, and be an unstoppable Warrior for God.

Choose Your Weapon

As the Battlefield Commander, you get to make the tough decisions. The decision to become a tither can be both easy and difficult. Deciding to tithe is easy when you know that it is what God asks you to do and out of love for Him and His kingdom, your desire is to become a giver.

It can also be difficult in that to some extent, we all like being in control of our money and keeping as much as we can. While the decision to tithe is a spiritual one, actually tithing is an act of the will that is cheered on by the heart. Become a cheerful giver or don't give at all.

Your final Battle Ready Training Task is to determine the size of your weapon. You have been given full authority to make the decision on how much and how frequently you will honor God with your tithes and offerings. Spend some time with your family and determine how much God is asking you to give.

Complete the following activities as you feel lead by the Holy Spirit:

- Spend time in prayer seeking God's direction on the amount you should give above your tithe of 10%

- Have your family members do the same

- Come together and discuss what the Lord has revealed to you each

- Decide on the amount and commit to actively tithe on all income you earn

- Trust God and His faithfulness to allow you to meet your needs with the remainder of your income

It is often said that the Checkbook is the last part of a believer that gets saved. While that is sort of funny to quote, it is a sad commentary on the state of today's church.

Learn to trust in God and His promises and then stand and lead the way for your family and your community. Bring the whole tithe into His house and watch Him do what only He can do.

Chapter 7

Take a Bow, Graduation Day is Here

"I am sure of this, that He who started a good work in you will carry it on to completion until the day of Christ Jesus." Philippians 1:6

If you are reading this, congratulations! You have made it. You stuck it out when things got tough, kept going when you wanted to quit, and have proven yourself worthy to be called a Financial Warrior. You have completed the training and have all that you need to win the battle for your finances.

Over the last six weeks, you have learned how to craft a Victor-Six-Vision to keep you moving in the right direction on the path to control your finances.

You have developed your very own Rules of Engagement that govern the way you handle money, the way you interact with other members of your team, and the way you handle your emotions and reactions to attacks.

You have been taught how to develop a Battle Ready Budget and have been given to tools to make it work. Knowing that your mission critical items are taken care of should give you peace of mind about managing your finances.

Savings is no longer a problem for you as you have found ways to reduce your household expenses, raise extra money, and automatically set aside funds to meet future needs.

You have a clear understanding of the uses and abuses of credit and know how to think critical and evaluate decisions pertaining to borrowing money.

Finally, you are prepared to unleash the power of the Tithe. You now know the results promised when you use this Secret Weapon and are prepared to receive the blessings of the Lord as you move forward in your financial future.

Wow! Looking back over the last 6 weeks, you have accomplished a lot. If you have followed along and completed the Battle Ready

Training Tasks, you have set yourself up to succeed. You are fully prepared to face all the enemy can throw at you.

As you go out from here, remember the things you have learned, hold onto your Victor-Six-Vision, and walk out your victory. You can do more than you think you can, be more than you think you are, and walk in the destiny God has for you.

Managing your finances well takes acting daily to make good decisions. Achieving substantial change in any area of life is most often a process and not an event.

Having read this book, you are now well equipped to make good decisions about your money and develop the habits that will take you where you want to go. The catch is that you have to remain vigilant and do the hard work of disciplining yourself to stay on the right track. It is very easy to get off course, get side tracked, get distracted, and end up in the same place you just fought to be free from.

Don't let that happen to you, as it has happened to me on more than one occasion. Having the information and knowing what to do are not the same as doing what needs to be done to win this fight.

Keep your Victor-Six-Vision ever before you, play by the Rules you have established, and use the Battle Ready Budget Tool to simplify the process. Start setting aside money for Emergency Expenses and Savings, even if it is a small amount to develop this valuable lifelong habit. Stay alert and be careful not to fall into the Credit/Debt Trap, and become a giver.

Trust God with your money will set you on the path to financial freedom faster than any other thing you will ever learn.

Your next step is to follow through and sign up for Battle Ready Finance: Advanced Training.

In this valuable resource, we will cover the challenging world of Investing; we will delve into company and personal Retirement Plans, and investigate ways to Save for College. We will discuss the impact Taxes have on your long term goals and dive into the concepts of Risk Management. Finally, we will cover Diversifying and Increasing Your Sources of Income.

Advanced Training is where the real work of creating Lifelong Wealth begins.

No longer do you have to be afraid of what may happen. You are ready. You are Battle Ready.

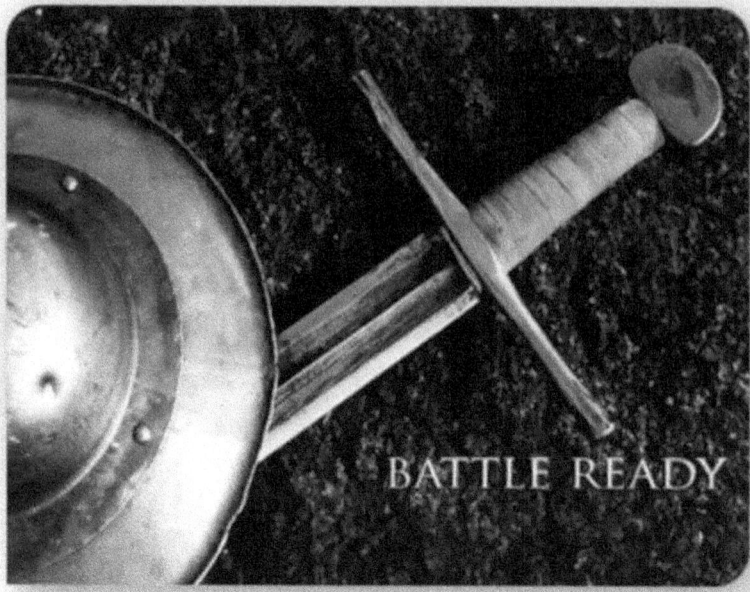

To receive your free Battle Ready Budgeting Tool, visit www.BattleReadyFinance.com

To purchase other books by J.W.Zinsmeister, visit our website at
www.battlereadyfinances.com
or check us out at Amazon.com.

Take advantage of the free calculators on our website and join our email list to stay up to date and be notified when the next book is published.

Appendix A: Firefight

At least once in every person's life comes a time when the need is great and the resources are few. It can be hard enough to make ends meet on a decent wage, but, when the times get tough and the money just is not there to meet the need, a person can easily despair.

If the battle is raging and you are in the middle of the fray and you feel like you are surrounded with no escape in site, take courage. There is glory yet to be had on this field. As long as you are alive to fight, all is not lost. There is a way out. It won't be easy, it won't be fun, but it can be done. Now it the time to keep your wits about you and come up with a new plan.

"We are hard pressed on every side, but not crushed; perplexed, but not in despair; persecuted, but not abandoned; struck down, but not destroyed". 2 Cor 4:8

Appendix A: Firefight has been written with you in mind. If you are constantly trying to come up with inventive ways to earn and save more, some of these suggestions may work for you. When you have good financial control and a good plan of action you can sleep better at night, knowing that the Cavalry Unit is set up to take care of Emergency needs.

There is no real magic formula for coming up with on-the-spot emergency cash. There is a good deal of thinking through and the putting of a good plan into action. If you can do that, you can make it work.

On the battlefield, if you can keep your head when everyone else is losing theirs, you will soon emerge as a natural leader. The ability to stay calm in a fight and manage your emotions is critical. If you are hit with a serious money crisis and you find yourself scrambling around for emergency money, follow the Battle Ready Warriors method to assess your situation and get back on your feet.

There are 4 steps:

1. Remain Calm

You must avoid giving in to crippling emotional setbacks. Stand strong in your faith. Regardless how bad things get, money problems can be solved with time and effort. You must prepare for the devastating fiscal and the emotional fallout that is sure to come when a financial crisis arises. You will need to cope very well with both if you hope to make a solid financial comeback.

Whenever a money emergency hits, it will be your ability to deal with the individual pitfalls that will hold you in good stead. It is when a series of financial hits come your way that the stress will tend to accumulate and make your life much more difficult to cope. Calm must take center stage. You must NEVER allow yourself the luxury of panic. This is your fight and there is no one to just take over. You are all you have. The more you panic, the less effective you will be. You need to keep a very clear head to be able to sit down and come up with an appropriate plan. Be aware of your own tendency to sabotage your plans further. It is only when you are at your most calm that you will be prepared to get to where you need to be and then overcome.

2. Evaluate the Damage

Make a clear assessment of your situation. You will not be so overwhelmed when you can calmly and rationally look at each individual problem as it arises. Don't bury your head in the sand. If you sit back wringing your hands with worry and allow all of your emergencies to pile into one, you may well find yourself down for the count. At even the first hint of a money emergency, it's important not to act right away.

Before you can manage your finances again, you have to first manage your emotions. You absolutely must regain your balance before you can even begin to make a plan. If your money emergency demands that you act quickly, think first about seeking the advice of a debt counselor, money coach or financial planner. If that is not possible, think about seeking out the aid of a financially perceptive friend or family member who can help you to come to a clearer perspective. Remember the old adage that "two heads are always better than one."

You won't need to make a major cash investment if you're strapped. Look for a planner who will give you a free one-hour consultation. Often times this will be all you will need to securely turn the corner.

Possibly one of the bigger mistakes people make when they're in a financial crisis is not being prepared to make a clear assessment of the damage. Denying there is an issue will only allow for more problems to occur. You can easily become overwhelmed.

However, totaling up the damage serves two important purposes. First, you need to know exactly how much you owe, how much money you have in hand, and what it will take to cover the distance between the two. Second, you will want to avoid any other mishaps, such as penalties, further repairs, missed deadlines, etc. Ideally, those unexpected expenses could be covered by the funds in the Cavalry Unit for Emergency Expenses.

The problem arises when the Cavalry Unit either is depleted or has not yet been funded.

3. Avoid Making Things Worse

When there are no emergency funds set aside, many people make the mistake of turning to credit cards for relief. Resist this one. You will only be transferring your problems from one pocket to the other. Relying on credit to fill in the gaps can be an okay one time solution, however, when it becomes habitual it will only add to your stress.

If you're truly running while on your last leg, you could consider taking out a home equity line of credit. This will work for some. The interest is tax deductible, and you can often get low fixed rates. Be smart about this remedy. Using your homes equity to fund your daily living expenses may work for a short time but just like credit cards, it adds to your overall debt load and adds to your stress level.

One source people often turn to is their company retirement plan. Think well before borrowing from your 401(k) or IRA. There are loopholes that allow you to do so, but there are also hidden costs—never mind potential taxes, penalties and other consequences. Keep in mind that if you were to lose your job, you'd have to repay the loan immediately, or be taxed as though it was a withdrawal. This remedy could be very costly in the long run.

4. Respond with Appropriate Force

While earning more income is the obvious solution to the problem, increasing your cash flow is not always easy. If there is no time or energy to take a second job and little hope for a raise, you may need to get really creative. Below are some ideas on ways to bring in more money:

- Offer a service. Can you walk a neighborhood dog, teach music lessons, or rake leaves? Is there opportunity to baby-sit for a friend, family, or neighbor? Can you do computer graphic design work, write bog posts, or design direct mail pieces? Consider which of your talents might be worth a few extra bucks and then search out individuals or businesses that are in need of those services. You may be able to earn some money while saving them a substantial amount.

- Take on a part-time job. Many people supplement their salaries with part-time retail jobs, especially during the holidays. Consider working the evening shift at a local retailer to bring in some extra funds. If you have reliable transportation, pizza delivery is also a popular choice for part time work.

- Borrow from a trusted friend or relative. The interest rate is low to nil, the cash is quick. Be sure you have a plan for how you're going to pay back the loan even before you approach them to avoid damaging the relationship due to a misunderstanding.

- Hold that "mother" of all garage sales, once and for all! Do your homework and literally do a house inventory. Journey back, all the way back, into the furthest reach of every closet and decide that, if you have not used it for more than six months, it will have to go. Most people have at least $1,000 worth of garage sale items hidden away in their home. This turns out to be a veritable gold mine for many.

- Determine who to pay and who to call. Sometimes hard decisions must be made. If that means letting your credit card bill go for a bit, so be it. As soon as you realize that you have a money emergency, contact your credit card issuers and request reduced interest rates and payments. Not only one, both. Let them know there is an emergency and see if they will work with you.

- For your car payment, call the creditor and request a payment extension. Perhaps you hate payment extensions, because they require a fee and you still have to make the payment at the end of the contract. In this case, a payment extension can allow a little breathing room to help you recover during your money emergency. Expect that you will likely have to pay a fee (usually about ¼ - 1/3 the car payment amount) for the extension. Freeing up the money you need today is your first and only goal at this point.

- Check to see if your mortgage holder will allow an extension for a nominal fee. Requesting an extension or an option to skip a payment may be just enough to get you past the emergency.

- Another quick fix is to host an online yard sale. Do a quick survey of your personal belongings. Come up with clothes that no longer fit, but that are in good condition, knick-knacks, dishes, electronics, gadgets, and books as well as stuff you bought but no longer use. Place free ads on

Craigslist or seek out local online sites. Many towns have these setup to allow for quick sales of unneeded items with little hassle.

- If you have a larger item to sell, call into the local radio stations to see if they have a "call in swap show" on the weekends. This is a very popular way to quickly convert gently used and more expensive items to fast cash. For things like cars and boats, Craigslist can be a good option, just beware of potential scammers.

Those 4 steps and the suggestions for raising quick funds my get you through a temporary emergency, but what if you have a bigger problem? What if your money woes are brought on not by a sudden emergency but a lifestyle of overspending and under earning? What do you do when you are at the point where your income can no longer match your expenses?

If that is where you find yourself, you can still follow the same 4 steps.

- Remain Calm.

- Evaluate the Damage.

- Avoid Making Things Worse.

- Respond with Appropriate Force.

When you realize that you are in trouble and things cannot continue down the same path, it is important to remain calm. The actions you take, regardless of what they are, will be more effective when you are not in a panicked state. Job interviews go much better when you are not desperately trying to get hired. Requests for loans to consolidate debt are much easy to get when you do not project your emotions onto the loan officer. Keep yourself in check and make rational decisions about your future.

Searching for and acquiring a new job or career has never been easier. Easier in the sense that jobs are searchable online, resumes can be submitted electronically, and first interviews can be conducted very quickly to see of the job is a good fit. If you find your income in not sufficient to meet the needs of your family, polish up your resume and see what is available.

When Evaluating the Damage, is it important to understand where you are financially and how you got there. This step is not to assign blame, but to prevent future mistakes. If it is a spending problem, consider selling things to recoup some of the costs and reduce debt. If it is an income problem, begin the job search in earnest and consider taking on a second job to help dig yourself out of the hole.

Regardless or your situation, you must develop a budget plan and an income plan. Once this step is complete, you can determine how much your income must increase or your spending must decrease.

Avoid Making Things Worse by stopping the behavior that has led to the problem. If you spend more than you make, stop immediately. Get on a budget and stick to it. If you cannot cut your fixed bills, you must eliminate some of your living expenses. Don't eat out, find and use coupons, and dine with family. Do whatever it takes to cut costs.

Once you have a handle on where you are, why you are there, and have stopped doing the things that got you there, decide how to Respond With Appropriate Force. Do you need to cut up credit cards? Should you go back to school? Can you take on extra shifts? Do you need a new career? Whatever is needed, you must be willing to act. Make the changes necessary to improve your situation.

The only way things will get better is if you take action. Spending time wondering why this has happened can be valuable for self-assessment, but must not be allowed to drag on continually.

Why you are here is not as important as how you will move forward. Bad things happen to good people every day. What matters is not what has happened, but how you respond to what has happened.

Financial stress is common among those forced into frugality because of a lost job, divorce, death in the family, or being overcome with debt, etc. This can cause you to feel insecure, fearful, anxious, angry, and depressed.

These same feelings are easily the number one cause of poor money management decisions. You must get your emotions under control. These poor decisions will lead to unmanageable debt loads, and start a vicious cycle of panic that never seems to end.

When you reach this point, and you find yourself with a money emergency, your feelings of helplessness can become so overwhelming you literally stop functioning in the real world.

If you recognize any of the above traits in yourself, get the help you need right away. See out a professional counselor ... talk to a friend or family member ... but talk to someone. If you know someone who is exhibiting the above traits, offer to help them. It doesn't matter whether you lend them cash, an ear, offer some helpful advice, or help them get counseling, just do something.

The first thing that you need to grasp is that no situation is hopeless. With just a little guidance and patience, along with a

couple of well thought out goals, and emotional support from family and friends, you can do what it takes to come out of dire circumstances.

You can adapt a new outlook, new skills, and best of all, a new feeling of self-esteem. Don't allow anyone to tell you different, and if they do, close the same door that they came into and don't again open it.

What you need is positive reinforcement and not negativity to help you get to the other side. Inside of you is a warrior and you need to embrace it.

You are more powerful than you know, more capable than you realize, and more resilient than you think. You can come back from this.

When you are desperate to raise emergency funds, it usually doesn't take very long for you to realize who really cares about you, who is truly a friend ... be they family or not. Your friends will be there for you in your time of need, offer encouragement, and lend an ear so you can just talk.

Ask for help in coming up with good ideas about how you can raise emergency funds during such a difficult time in your life. Be open to the many suggestions that you will receive.

There may come the time when you will need to put aside your emotions and just concentrate on the wellbeing of you and your family. This has to be your priority during times of financial stress and upheaval.

In financially stressful times, if you, as the Mom or Dad, can't cope, how can you expect your children to cope now, or in the future? You must set the example for the rest of the family to draw strength from them.

So make the decision today to learn how to cope, to make the changes you can, to stay focused and goal-oriented, and to let anxiety and financial stress go out the door so that you will be prepared to deal with any money emergencies that come your way.

"I have told you these things so that in Me you may have peace. You will have suffering in this world. Be courageous! I have conquered the world." John 16:33

Suggestions for Savings

If you are currently not in a Firefight but want to increase your cash flow to be prepared when the bullets start to fly, consider adopting some of the following habits:

- The next time you treat yourself or your family to a meal out, tip yourself! Just as you go to tip the waitress 15 to 20 percent, put the same amount aside for yourself. When you get home, stash it away in your cookie jar. Every time you go through a fast food window, put a dollar away for that cookie jar.

- When using cash, never spend anything smaller than a $5. Everything smaller goes into a container. Put aside a large envelope, cookie tin, coffee jar or something similar. By the end of your first month you should have some extra cash put aside to have a nice start on an emergency fund. Don't count it or spend it but place it somewhere that is hidden away. At the end of each month, put it somewhere that you won't be tempted to dip into it. This kind of money really adds up.

- The next time you get a good raise, instead of applying it to your cost of living, bank it. This way you will always be living one raise behind and your bank account will be growing by some 3 percent.

- Take advantage of that cash back option. Next time you make a purchase using your debit card, ask for a small amount of cash back. Instead of spending it, stash it away in your cookie jar. Chances are you won't even miss that extra $1, $2 or $5 bill and come emergency time, you will notice how the amount has piled up.

- Next time you pay off that big-ticket item like a new car or tuition, continue to make the payments to yourself. Set up a savings account and each month slip the ghost payment into it. Watch as it builds nicely.

- If you have noticed that you can get a better long distance telephone plan and you want to switch, allocate the savings to your cookie jar. You won't likely miss that little bit of extra money, and you will have a better telephone plan.

- Sign up for a grocery shopping membership card. At the bottom of your store receipt, you will see a print out that states how much you save each week. It really adds up. You can easily save an average of $15 on each weekly grocery trip. Add that amount, each week, to your savings cookie jar.

- Did you enjoy your tax refund this year? Sure you did, we all did. That's because of the new tax laws. Many people will have a little extra money coming their way after April 15. Decide to deposit that extra money right away into your savings account or cash it and then stash it. Sure you can come up with plenty of ways you can use that money now, but put it away for later.

- At the end of each workday simply empty your pockets or clean out your change purse. All the change goes into the jar. Who wants to carry around all that dead weight, anyway? Your spare change adds up a lot faster than you think. While you are at it, add at least one bill to your change jar at the end of each week. Aim for a $20.

- Is it time to give up that nasty smoking habit? Imagine the money you will save. If you are not quite ready to quit at least cut back by half. Put the savings each day into your change jar and watch it overflow.

- If you yearn to lose some weight, try rewarding yourself the cost of the item that you do without each day. Put that money into your change jar. You will look great and you will be saving for a rainy day.

- When mortgage rates are especially low—consider refinancing your mortgage and, while you're at it, your car loans, too.

- When you live in an area that has good public transportation, see if you can get by on one car instead of two.

- Make your current car last. With good maintenance, you will be able to replace it every six to eight years instead of every three years.

- Do a periodical energy check on the house. Replace all essentials such as cracked storm windows and renew the weather stripping.

- Cancel subscriptions to magazines or newspapers that you're not reading.

- Eat out less often and learn to be creative using leftovers. If you stop for a morning cup of coffee at the local Deli, make coffee at home.

- For the kids weekly allowance cut it back. Explain to them that every member of the family needs to contribute to the emergency fund for it to work.

- Spend less money than you earn each week. Seek out a higher paying job. Keep your job skills sharp and up-to-date so that when a new opportunity comes up, you will be on your toes and first in line.

- Adjust your lifestyle to always spend a bit less. Create a firm financial budget to encourage saving. If you must use credit cards/cut up those you can do without.

- If you must use credit cards, pay them all down in full each month. If you have credit card debt at high rates, consolidate at once.

- Figure out a way to lower your student loan payments.

- Just say NO to spending money whenever possible.

- Lower your expenses, one by one.

- Stop purchasing items that you can do without.

- Forgo purchasing non-essential items.

- Refinance your mortgage or debt at a much lower rate.

- Refinance your car loan at a much lower interest rate.

- Find cheaper insurance rates then switch over.

- Use coupons to shop with. Don't purchase without a discount coupon.

- Wait for things to first go on sale before buying.

- Take advantage of catalog saving certificates.

- Don't buy an item just because it is on sale.

- Buy generic or non-name brand merchandise as much as possible.

- Wait for prices to fall to a discounted rate before buying (applies especially to electronics items).

- Reward yourself for saving money. Enjoy as your debt shrinks and your investments grow.

- Drive used cars or leases rather than brand new cars.

- Reduce your auto insurance.

- Don't eat out as much as you'd like to.

- If you do eat out, buy gift certificates for half price meals.

- Buy only discount magazines.

- Do more stay in activities at home.

- Invest the money you save to earn even more.

- Create a plan to save $200 each month (as much as you can manage.) Never miss the monthly savings payment to yourself and try to find ways to increase it.

- Don't spend money just because you have it.

- Look into getting a better quality education.

- Stay very busy – you will have less time to spend money. Find an interesting hobby to occupy your time and stop you from spending.

- Find a hobby that you can turn into earnings.

- Stop smoking and bank the savings.

- Go on a sensible diet and lose weight. You will save money on food, look and feel better, and your long-term healthcare costs should fall dramatically.

- Learn how to manage your finances by reading financial publications.

- Increase the amount of money you earn through a second job, promotion, new job, investments, etc.

- Don't try to compete with your friends and neighbors. Be satisfied with what you have.

- Don't compare yourself to your friends and neighbors. Be happy being you.

- Sell your car and take the bus to work if you can.

- Contribute the maximum each year to your 401K or to an IRA.

- Paying down your debt is also a way to save money (it saves you from a debt payment and brings you closer to having money to invest).

- Lower your cable bill by deleting pay channels or switch to satellite.

- Earn extra money by completing short surveys online.

- Practice restraint at all times.

- Be patient when bargain shopping.

- Shop for clothing at thrift shops (especially for young kids). Look for gently worn or even new clothes for 1/10 the price of new (or less).

- Put your kids on the school bus rather than driving them to school.

- Slipcover or reupholster older furniture for a quick update rather than buying expensive new furniture.

- Refinish furniture and/or decorate with new paint.

- Use older and broken furniture to make a unique piece.

- Take your lunch to work every day!

- Make your meals in bulk and then freeze them in smaller containers to save even more money.

- Buy a bread maker to make your own bread. This is much cheaper than $2.00 a loaf, and tastes terrific!

- Shop for dented canned goods and outdated toiletries at salvage grocery stores.

- Read magazine subscriptions at the library or buy them at the thrift shop for .25 to .50 after someone else has read them.

- Stop drinking expensive sodas and make Kool-Aid, or decaffeinated iced tea, or water instead.

- Cancel expensive telephone options like call waiting.

- Check out library books instead of buying expensive new titles.

- Change your eating habits and avoid expensive, processed foods.

- Exercise and eat right to keep your doctor bills down.

- Brush and floss your teeth to keep the dentist bill down.

- Keep up on regular auto maintenance and avoid costly repair.

- Mend your clothing instead of buying new clothes.

- Buy only clothing that does not require dry cleaning.

- Take care of your own nails. Avoid manicures.

- Simplify your hairstyle – wear a hairdo that doesn't require much maintenance.

- Get at least 3-6 quotes when shopping for items over $100.

- Develop self-control and simplify your life if possible.

- Buy only inexpensive, no-name drugstore cosmetics.

- Cut your dryer sheets in half.

- Buy generic over the counter medicine rather than name brand items when possible.

- Buy generic baby wipes, diapers, and formula, anything you can for the baby.

- Look for quality, name brand clothing at garage sales in more affluent neighborhoods.

- Find fashionable clothing in the sale departments of stores like the Gap and Stitches.

- Keep in fashion by finding basic colored tees and skirts and then add cheaper, trendy accessories.

- Buy baby clothes privately from someone that has an older child (one year older) than yours. You can find good quality clothing cheaper this way.

- When you get change back from a purchase put it in the piggy bank. Always give the cashier whole dollars, not the exact amount. In a few months, you will have "found" money that can be used for an emergency fund.

- You can save money by shopping for groceries in the "bulk foods" aisles in your grocery store.

- Layer up in the wintertime. You don't need the heat above 68 degrees in the winter inside your house. Wear warm clothes and socks/slippers while in the house.

- Use all plastic bags you receive at the grocery store for trash bags.

- Some grocery stores give you a 5-cent credit per bag if you bring your own bags. Pennies add up over time.

- Breastfeed your children!

- Save money when shopping next time at the supermarket by remembering to check the lower items nearer to floor level as they are often much cheaper than those at eye level.

- Also, resist the temptation to purchase extra items at the checkout such as magazines and candy bars.

- When you receive a gift that you are sure you won't use, re-gift! The next time you will need to buy a gift – give away one of your own.

- Buy, slaughter and butcher your own cow. The average cost of the meat is $1.00 per pound.

- Hand-pick your own fruits and vegetables in season. They are less expensive and better quality foods.

- The next time you yearn to see a movie wait to see it on DVD at the video store.

- Quick braking, cornering, and accelerating (speeding) will eat your gas up considerably.

- Never let your fuel needle go below a ½ tank, or fill it up when you drive it to "Empty".

- Instead of buying a new DVD, save money by trading with family and friends. Once a month do the rounds and before you know it, you will have a new library of good movies to enjoy.

- Plant a small garden each spring, with just the vegetables that you really like. Even a small effort every day can save you dollars usually spent on fresh vegetables at the produce market.

- Buy your bread and other bakery items at the local thrift bread store.

- Check your local library for the newest DVD/video releases and then rent three for $2.00 for two days.

- Read your local newspapers online.

- Search eBay for big ticket items and then save literally hundreds on computers, DVD players, etc.

- Keep track of the cost of items you buy a lot and get them at the cheapest store, like cleaning supplies at Family Dollar, pet food at Wal-Mart, etc.

- Make a conscious effort to combine tasks that require driving some place, so you will get the most out of your mileage.

- Stop buying gifts. For your friends and family who do not feel slighted by this, send e-mail cards for holidays, birthdays and as thank you cards.

- In addition, e-mail family and friends who live far away, instead of calling long distance.

- Get rid of your monthly fee long distance service, and just use an access code when you do call, which is infrequently anyway and inexpensive.

- Decide which satellite channels you could do without, and give up a few shows you really like. You can save more than $20.00 on your monthly bill.

- When you buy vegetables, fruits and bread at the grocery store check the reduced-for-quick-sale carts and shelves first.

- Change the oil in your vehicles yourself.

- Save money when buying clothes for the following year at the end of the season / during the off season. You can get great mark down prices.

- Each evening take the spare change from your pockets or periodically clean out your purse and toss the coins aside. Never take any money back until the end of the year. Then take all of the coins to the bank and exchange them for cash.

- You'll be surprised to find out they've added up to $50, $100 or even $200.

- Shop garage sales for a great source of household items, books, clothing, and furniture.

- Don't buy bottled water! Buy a good water-filter and drink tap water.

There are literally hundreds of suggestions for ways to save money. Make it fun and become as frugal as possible. See it as a game and get the whole family involved. It's you and your family in a fight against the enemy. Recruit them in the fight and take back your finances.

If you find cutting expenses and saving money to be a difficult thing to do, go back to Chapter 1 and revisit your Victor-Six-Vision. Make sure that you create a personal vision that is strong enough to get you through the tough battles you will encounter as you begin to be a saver. By taking control of your finances, you are slapping the enemy in the face. You can rest assured that he will increase the attacks to try and break your will. Don't give in. *"Resist the devil and he will flee from you"*. This is a fight you can win. It will take clear vision, a calm resolve, and dedication on everyone's part, but you can do it. You are not fighting alone and the Lord has given you this promise to hold onto: *"The Lord will cause the enemies who rise up against you to be defeated before you. They will march out against you from one direction but flee from you in seven directions."* Deut. 28:7

Stand and fight, regain control of your finances, and walk in the freedom that God has for you!

Index

A

B

C

D

E

F

H

I

L

M

R

S

T

V

www.ingramcontent.com/pod-product-compliance
Lightning Source LLC
Chambersburg PA
CBHW031956190326
41520CB00007B/270